THE BIBLICAL THEOLOGY
OF THE SECULAR

THE BIBLICAL THEOLOGY OF THE SECULAR is one of the IMPACT BOOKS, a series designed to bring the modern reader the significant achievements of scholars, both Catholic and non-Catholic, in the fields of Scripture, Theology, Philosophy, Mathematics, History, and the Physical and Social Sciences. Among the titles in the series are:

The
Biblical Theology
of the
Secular

GEORGE T. MONTAGUE, S.M.

THE BRUCE PUBLISHING COMPANY / MILWAUKEE

IMPRIMI POTEST:

REV. Q. HAKENEWERTH, S.M.
Censor deputatus

NIHIL OBSTAT:

RICHARD J. SKLBA, S.S.L., S.T.D.
Censor librorum

IMPRIMATUR:

✠ WILLIAM E. COUSINS
Archbishop of Milwaukee
October 5, 1967

Library of Congress Catalog Card Number: 68–14112

Copyright © 1968 THE BRUCE PUBLISHING COMPANY

MADE IN THE UNITED STATES OF AMERICA

Foreword

The following essays were originally written as lectures for the Chicago Biblical Institute in the summer of 1967. With slight modifications they are presented here as a contribution to the current discussion on the theology of the secular in a style which, it is hoped, will make the matter accessible to the interested non-specialist. The study is obviously not a definitive one; it will have achieved its purpose if it succeeds in raising and clearly formulating the questions urged upon us by the biblical materials themselves.

George T. Montague, S.M.
St. Mary's University

Contents

THE BIBLICAL THEOLOGY
OF THE SECULAR

1. Early Pentateuchal Motifs

When the "Death of God" theologians made their spectacular debut on the contemporary stage, Catholics generally considered their debates to be intramural among Protestants. With a certain amount of detached curiosity, Catholics either identified the movement as the swan-song of a decadent theology, or at best considered this sudden piping of optimism about the world as a reaction to Protestantism's too-long-sung dirge over the depravity of man and nature. Catholics wondered whether the world, which had not wept at the dirge, might dance to the piping.

But then it became evident that the problem was not confined to the Protestant camp, as Leslie Dewart showed in *The Future of Belief.* It is the serious problem of the relevance of Christian faith in terms of the experience of modern man and the pressing need for the Church to understand, first of all, and then to communicate the faith in terms of man's common experience today.

Harvey Cox, it will be remembered, devoted some initial pages of *The Secular City* to the biblical theology of the secular, and Van Buren has written a book called *The Secular Meaning of the Gospel.* But as far as I know, there has been no comprehensive study made on the biblical theology of the secular — and certainly not by Catholics.

Yet the need for such a study is imperative. Many of the theologians preoccupied with these problems are not biblical specialists. Mascall, for one, admits as he begins his work on *The Secularization of Christianity* (p. x) that he is "less at home" in this area. Nevertheless, he points up the need for such a study when he says that Van Buren speaks only of the

1

secularization of theology because he has no theology of the secular (p. 44).

The present essay makes no pretense of being a comprehensive study of the question. It is rather an attempt to uncover the building blocks for a biblical theology of the secular. Immediately, of course, one will see the vastness of the subject and the near gratuitousness of the approach — it all depends on what we mean by *secular*.

The semantics of the problem have been analyzed by Father Thomas Clarke.[1] After discussing the various ways in which terms like "secular," "sacred," "religious" and "holy" are used, he offers a simple division between the "secular," which defines man's relation to the world, and the "religious," which defines his relation to God. The *religious* he subdivides into "the saintly," which implies no idea of separateness, and "the sacred" which does. With this division he seeks to do justice to the very real areas of man's life which are not "set aside" from the secular and yet are truly "religious" in the sense that they are, in their very secularity, an important element in the Christian's life synthesis. The sacred continues to play an important role both in the life of the individual Christian and in the life of the Christian community. The problem seems to be to properly relate the two — to avoid the extreme of totally identifying one with the other and yet to discover the relevance of one to the other. The nexus of relevance seems to be what is so obscure today. The wag who said, "God is not dead; he just doesn't want to get involved," may have been expressing a theological absurdity or at least a caricature of the Christian God. But the fact is that many "exemplary" Christians do present such an image to the world — as I became aware of one morning this past year when I saw that very witticism scrawled in two-foot letters along the side of a religious house in San

---

[1] Thomas E. Clarke, S.J., "What is Secular Christianity?" in *Proceedings of the Twenty-First Annual Convention, The Catholic Theological Society of America* (Yonkers, N. Y.: St. Joseph's Seminary, 1966), pp. 201–221.

Antonio. And many, especially among the "radical" theologians, have become so impatient with the seeming irrelevance of religion as to cry for a total secularization of Christianity as soon as possible. Related to this problem of relevance is the fact that the world has reached a certain autonomy from religion, what many have called a "coming of age." This process has been going on for centuries, but its acceleration in the last decades has been phenomenal. What does Scripture have to say, if anything, about this problem?

Scripture has been invoked to support every imaginable thesis. It has surely, in the course of Christian history, been invoked to justify a retreat from the world. And I am afraid from the outset that my way of defining the secular may have committed me to the same methodological error of searching the Scriptures for a justification of a this-worldly involvement. I hope this is not so. To avoid that pitfall, I have sought to treat the subject in historical context, beginning with the earliest documents of the Old Testament and tracing the theme through the New Testament. I might say from the outset that we should not be surprised to find some lack of consistency in the attitude of Scripture toward the world, precisely because we do find conflicting theologies in both the Old Testament and the New — and nowhere perhaps is the conflict so intense as in the sacred writers' interpretation of "this worldly events." The fact, however, that conflicting tensions were accepted into the sacred tradition of God's people indicates that they felt that somehow these tensions were or could be resolved in a higher synthesis — a tendency which the growth of the scriptural corpus itself illustrates.

This point is worth stressing at the outset. Any universalizing of a scriptural affirmation or drawing a contemporary application from it is justified only if we fully understand the historical context in which it was first uttered or written. Otherwise, we run the great risk of making Scripture say more — or less —than it is actually saying. But from such a study, far from finding our contemporary concern hemmed in by a biblical literalism, we discover precisely the freedom it gives us to solve today's problems in the light of the Spirit in the Church today.

If we do not forget that we enjoy a solidarity in faith with Abraham and all succeeding generations of believers, then our communing with them in this research can only lead to a strengthening of that faith in us today and a courageous moving forward into the unknown terrain of the next decades into which the God of Abraham is leading us.

For all that, it is not an easy task to determine the date of many scripture passages, realizing, as we must, that the passage in question may have circulated orally for centuries before it was written down. And then in the course of the years, there was an editing and new application of many passages to new situations. What follows is then only a selection of the most salient scripture passages.

I. THE REVELATION OF THE DIVINE NAME
(Exodus 3:13–14)

Where does the Bible really begin? The opening passage about creation in Genesis, the Priestly account, dates from the exile; it was obviously meant to be a preface to the story of God's deeds of salvation. The whole first eleven chapters of Genesis, in fact, though of very ancient tradition, were intended as a prelude to the history of the Chosen People. The stories of the patriarchs, while also very ancient, were apparently preserved and developed around the cultic centers of the land of Canaan after the conquest. So one is hard put to determine where a study like ours should start. I have decided to start with what in Jewish tradition turned out to be a most central event: the Exodus and the Covenant — and first of all, the revelation of the divine name (or lack of it) to Moses.

> Then Moses said to God, "I am to go, then, to the sons of Israel and say to them, 'The God of your fathers has sent me

to you.' But if they ask me what his name is, what am I to tell them?" And God said to Moses, "I Am Who I Am. This," he added, "is what you must say to the sons of Israel: 'I Am has sent me to you'" (Ex 3:13–14).*

There is still a great amount of dispute among scholars as to the meaning of the name Yahweh and of the meaning of the present text, which apparently wishes to give an explanation of it: *"Ehyeh asher ehyeh"* ("I Am Who I Am"). Whatever the name Yahweh originally meant (and evidence is strong that it goes back beyond Hebrew to an Amoritic or some other northwestern Semitic dialect), the Hebrew understanding of it as given in our present text is theologically crucial. One thing is generally admitted by all: the Greek idea of subsistent being, though finding some justification in the Septuagint rendering *ego eimi ho ōn,* is far from both the etymology of the Hebrew and the Israelites' understanding of their God. The verb *to be* in Hebrew is not the simple copulative which it can be in English — it has an active sense: "to become, take place, come to pass, be present." Hence, even etymologically, the sense of the expression "I am" is "I am here and ready to act." The usage of the divine name elsewhere in the book of Exodus confirms this dynamic meaning of the name. In the context of the plague narratives we read: "I will lay my hand on Egypt. . . . And all the Egyptians shall come to know that I am Yahweh when I stretch out my hand against Egypt and bring out the sons of Israel from their midst" (Ex 7:4–5), or again: "But I shall set apart the land of Goshen, where my people live, on that day; there will be no gadflies there, and so you may know that I, Yahweh, am in the midst of the land (of Egypt)" (Ex 8:18) — that is, you will know that I am present and active and that there are no territorial limits to my power. Even more cryptically, in Exodus 6:6 ff., the divine name is immediately followed by a series of promised events which

* Unless otherwise indicated, all biblical citations are taken from *The Jerusalem Bible* © 1966 by Darton, Longman and Todd, Ltd. and Doubleday, Inc. Reprinted by permission.

explain the significance of the mysterious expression: "I am Yahweh. I will free you of the burdens which the Egyptians lay on you. I will release you. . . . I will adopt you as my own people. . . . You will know that it is I, Yahweh your God, who have freed you from the Egyptians' burdens. Then I will bring you into the land. . . ." Using the same terminology, Hosea will reverse the process later, when he says, "You are not my people, and I will *not be* to you" (*weanoki lo ehyeh lakem*) (Hos 1:8–9, my translation).

Yahweh is thus telling Moses and his people: "You will know who I am from experiencing what I do for you." This type of revelation is interesting from several points of view. First, it is clearly a refusal to adopt or accept a name that has any specific conceptual value. The later interdiction of images is but a consequence of this unconceptualized formulation of the divine name. Yahweh was not to be tied to any specific created image. Second, if it is true that in ancient times to know the name of a being was to have power over it, by this revelation Yahweh makes clear that he will not permit man to imagine that he can control his God, or box him within human projects, so that at a magical pronouncing of a name, man might be able to have a miraculous future at his will.[2] Although this is certainly not an affirmation of the widespread modern conviction that man's destiny is wholly in his own hands, it nevertheless does imply a weaning of man from the infantile fantasy that somehow he can have an easy and irresponsible way out of his existential predicament by invoking a supernatural intervention tailored to his whims.

Even God's revelation of what he is going to do next does not imply an abdication of his freedom. It is precisely this which is implied in the expression "I Am who I Am" — i.e.,

---

[2] In the last years before the exile Israel had veered away from this notion of God's personal transcendence and had begun to assume that Yahweh was just like the pagan gods, impersonal powers out of personal contact with man and always subject to incantations of human ritual: cf., e.g., the thrice repeated "The temple of the Lord" (Jer 7:4).

"I shall act where I shall act," which Father Plastaras glosses thus: "I will be present (in a dynamic, active sense) wherever, whenever, and to whomever I will be present."[3] There is no magic hold man can get on Yahweh; no secret passage to the divine intelligence or will; no cryptic or magical formula which can contain him. In this, Mosaic religion transcended its surrounding religions. God is God and not man. We are on the road to understanding the transcendence of God and to realizing that only when God is God can man be man. The horizon of the present text, however, presents this truth in a more simple light: if God's presence (I avoid the more Greek-sounding "immanence") is revealed in historical deeds, his transcendence is revealed in the freedom and gratuity with which these are performed.

A third important element in this revelation is that God's self-revelation remains open-ended and pointing toward the future. The name is a promise of a continuing revelation. God refuses to reveal himself fully at this moment, but directs the attention of his people to the events of their coming history as the medium through which they will come ever better to understand who Yahweh is. Thus the very divine name turns the attention of the people to a this-worldly realization, a this-worldly involvement, and a future that is not mythical but historical.

II. THE COVENANT (Exodus 19)

The fact that emerges as truly unique about ancient Israel's constitution as a people — and therefore about her cult — is that the instrument chosen to express her relationship with her God was not something directly religious but rather something of the political order. It was an instrument of relationships between men, between kings or peoples, the suzerainty treaty by which a Lord-King would establish a covenant with a vassal to stabilize and secure their future

---

[3] *The God of Exodus* (Milwaukee: The Bruce Publishing Company, 1966), p. 98.

relationships. Like everything of public interest in the ancient world, of course, the gods were introduced into the treaties, but only as witnesses of the agreement, as its executors — to bless the contractants if they kept it, to punish them if they defaulted. But essentially the instrument was a political one, hardly suited, it would seem, to describe the relation of a people with a god. For most of the ancient gods were nature gods; and what was crucial for man was, through cultic acts, to get a sufficient hold on his god to guarantee fertility and prosperity during the coming year. If this alone could be achieved, one could be certain of the future. If the god acts favorably at all, it can only be in one direction, the only change being the renewal of nature (which is no real change at all).

A covenant of the Sinai type, however, expressed a completely different type of relationship. As a political instrument, it was based on Yahweh's past saving deeds in the political and historical order rather than in the order of nature; and the future was as free and undetermined as historical action might warrant. Moreover, conditions were unilaterally imposed not on God but on the people. Here was a people bound to a King they could not see, of whom there was to be not even an image, who scarcely had a name — and yet in that name they were willing to accept severe moral demands which no other god made on his people.

The use of a political instrument as the means of God's self-revelation meant a greater stress both on the *presence* of God to the daily life of the people and on his *free transcendence*. It meant a greater presence to the daily life of the people, because by the covenant *everything* in the life of Israel was sacralized. "You of all the nations shall be my very own; for all the earth is mine. I will count you a kingdom of priests, a consecrated nation" (Ex 19:5b–6).[4]

---

[4] This text justifies a distinction such as that offered by Father Clarke between that which falls in the sphere of the divine without being separated (the "saintly") and that which falls in the sphere of the divine by reason of a special separation or consecration (the "sacred").

In the ancient world, the king held dominion over the entire kingdom, but he had direct ownership only over certain limited possessions, which were his *segullāh*. So likewise, the national god (like Ba'al Melqart of the Phoenicians) exercised dominion over the entire kingdom but his *segullāh* was limited to his sanctuary, his holy mountain. What Yahweh affirms in the above text is that the whole earth is his kingdom, and that the people of Israel constitute his *segullāh* within that kingdom. The significance of this affirmation is expressed by Father Plastaras in this way:

> Israel, in responding to God's word, has entered into a new sphere of existence. There could no longer be a radical separation between the sacred and the profane in the life of this people. The community which came into existence at Sinai was essentially a worshiping community, but their service of Yahweh could not be restricted to cult. Every phase of Israel's life — social, military, political and family institutions — would have to bear witness to the world concerning the revelation.[5]

At this point of our inquiry, then, it seems infelicitous to say that Israelite religion represented a de-sacralization of politics — although Harvey Cox makes perfectly clear what he means by using the term. It is more exact to say that everything was sacralized — that whereas religion was limited among the pagan nations to the sphere of cult and cultic acts, in Israelite religion the sacred was extended beyond cult to everything in human life, and, first of all to man's moral life, his relation to his fellow man. Henceforth, therefore, the secular could never be a matter of indifference in Israelite religion. Man could not be a split personality, living in two unrelated worlds — that of religion and that of daily life — for Yahweh had consecrated *everything* in the life of his people. It will be the task of the prophets to hammer home the lesson in the centuries to come, and this is the lesson which the Epistle of John will echo in New Testament times: "Anyone who says, 'I love God,' and hates his brother, is a liar" (1 Jn 4:20).

---

[5] *Ibid.*, p. 224.

This greater sense of God's presence to all the activities of life went hand in hand with a more exalted idea of his transcendence. As more than one scholar has remarked, the holy of holies in Israel was not, as in Phoenician temples, the place where the sacred image of God was kept away from profane gaze. It was an empty room. Because God is not localized, he can be found everywhere.

Once again we find that the use of a secular instrument to express God's relationship with his people directed their attention to the importance of daily human activity as the sphere where man meets God.

III. THE BATTLE SONGS

The oldest elements in the Pentateuch are poetry. And among the poems, a significant place is occupied by the songs that celebrate the victory of the God of battles. Scholars generally agree that the refrain of the victory canticle in Exodus 15 probably dates back to the time of the event itself, whereas the rest is merely a later liturgical expansion: "It was then that Moses and the sons of Israel sang this song in honour of Yahweh: 'Yahweh I sing: he has covered himself in glory, horse and rider he has thrown into the sea'" (Ex 15:1, 2). Another example of these refrains is that over Amalek: "Lay hold of the banner of Yahweh! Yahweh is at war with Amalek from age to age!" (Ex 17:16.) The Canticle of Deborah in Judges 5 fits the same pattern. It is the magnificent victory song composed after the Israelites' striking triumph over the Canaanite armies in the valley of Jezreel.

One of the first ways, then, in which Yahweh reveals himself is by victory on the battlefield. Or, as Exodus 15:3 puts it, "Yahweh is a warrior." He has the power to win victories (1 Sam 17:47), and the battle cry is "Yahweh is lord of the battle" (*ibid.*). The concept of the Holy War was a common one among ancient peoples. In Israel, it was understood to be an integral part of covenant theology. If Yahweh was the God of his people, he would fight for them.

Viewed from our modern perspective, this conception of a warrior-God may seem quite primitive. Even more primitive, and by contemporary standards, incomprehensible, are the consequences drawn from this for the cities that fell to the Israelites' sword in the promised land — the *herem* (cf. Jos 6:21; 8:26, 28; 9:24; 10:28–43). A God who would decree the complete destruction of man and beast by the victors seems, by contemporary standards, hardly a God of mercy and justice.

We could, of course, just write off the Holy War as one of those provisional things of the Old Testament that would be replaced by the more perfect teaching and example of Jesus. However, lest we miss what is perennially valuable in these passages, a few remarks are in order.

First, and perhaps most important, we must distinguish at each stage of revelation what could be called the formal aspect of revelation and the material context in which it is revealed. When the lights are brought onto a dark stage gradually by a rheostat, the earliest shapes that the viewer sees are only the beginning of a true perspective. Or, to vary the image, the peaks one sees at close range as he climbs a mountain may loom very large; once one has reached the summit, he sees them in a perspective balanced by the whole panorama.

Now the cultural context in which the fierce monotheism of Yahwistic faith emerged was one that thought of war not only as just and permissible at times, but even as a holy thing. A God who, more than any other nation's god, had proclaimed himself to be *with* his people, to make their future his own, could not possibly be conceived, in the context of the thirteenth century B.C., as anything *but* a warrior God. National survival and "salvation" could simply not be conceived in other terms. Otherwise God would really have been "dead" — and this was just what Israel came to believe about the idols of the pagans. Israel's God, on the other hand, was a *living* God — and living meant active and committed and involved. This is forcefully brought out in Psalm 115:3–8:

> Ours is the God whose will is sovereign
> in the heavens and on earth,
> whereas their idols, in silver and gold,
> products of human skill,
>
> have mouths, but never speak,
> eyes, but never see,
> ears, but never hear,
> noses, but never smell,
>
> hands, but never touch,
> feet, but never walk,
> and not a sound from their throats.
> Their makers will end up like them,
> and so will anyone who relies on them.

However, even within this cultural context, there were some significant aspects of the Yahweh-warrior theme that pointed beyond mere military conquest. In the Yahwist-Elohist account of the Exodus (which was always considered to be a prototype of the Holy War), there is a strong emphasis not only on the lack of military arms among the refugees (which was probably the real historical situation) but also on their uselessness, and the importance of leaving the entire victory to Yahweh. "Have no fear! Stand firm, and you will see what Yahweh will do to save you today; the Egyptians you see today, you will never see again. Yahweh will do the fighting for you; you have only to keep still!" (Ex 14:13 f.)

This theme appears repeatedly, especially later in the prophetic literature, and while at times, the Hebrews' military might may be described, the ideal of the Holy War always seems to have been one in which the entire initiative and responsibility is left to Yahweh himself, and in this sense numbers and power can even be an obstacle (Gideon, Jgs 7; 1 Sam 14:6). In the Exodus, the ideal of the Holy War was achieved, for there Israel remained perfectly passive and dependent upon Yahweh for its deliverance. If this theology were pursued to its logical conclusions, says Father Plastaras, it would have led to complete pacifism. But it would take the voice of prophets like Isaiah and Jeremiah to drive the lesson home that what God expected of his people was in the first place a trust in him and an observance of his law, and that military and political intrigue was suicidal if (as happened) it came to replace the covenant-law.

Beyond this, the very motif of the Holy War, with Yahweh as Warrior, became one of the sharpest tools later turned by the prophets on the people themselves to awaken them to the sense of sin. Yahweh, they would dare to proclaim, is the general of the *foreign* armies (cf. Jer 50:9; Is 41:2, 25; 43:17; Ez 26:7; 28:7):[6] Assyria is the rod of his wrath (Is 10:5); he sends the fire of judgment in a military invasion (Am 1:3–2:5). This incomprehensible reversal of the role of Yahweh warrior would never have been so agonizing had not Israel been radically convinced that Yahweh was *her* warrior God. A military invasion or defeat for Israel did not mean that the foreign gods had overpowered Yahweh, but that Yahweh himself found something inimical to him in his own people. Thus the very concept of Yahweh as a warrior god turned out to be a first stepping-stone to a purer conception of God as the one who will be what he will be, and raised the question as to what it really was in his people that he was warring for.

The third phenomenon to observe in connection with the Holy War was the religious dedication that it evoked. In the period of the Judges, which marked the apogee of Holy War theology, the men who served under the charismatic leaders were considered "consecrated" and "holy" persons for the whole duration of the war (1 Sam 21:14; Is 13:3). An absolute single-mindedness was demanded of them. The

---

[6] Cf. Henning Fredricksson, *Jahwe als Krieger, Studien zum alttestament-lichen Gottesbild* (Lund, 1945), pp. 23–27. For the battle-motif turned against Jerusalem extensively in Lamentations cf. Norman K. Gottwald, *Studies in the Book of Lamentations* (London: SCM Press, 1962), pp. 85 f.

fearful, the newly-married, and those entangled in financial
or domestic worries were invited by the commanding officers
to go home (Dt 20:49). Their presence in the army would
break the unity of those who "offered themselves willingly"
(Jgs 5:2). A man who had sexual intercourse with a woman
was disqualified from entering the encampment and pursuing
the war (1 Sam 21:4; 2 Sam 11:11), a practice we see
observed as late as Davidic times when Uriah refused, on
leave, to go home to his wife. This religious element is
important as laying an early foundation for the eschatological
significance of celibacy in New Testament times.

What, then, can be drawn of value today from the theology
of the Holy War? Granted that it was reinterpreted in the
New Testament in terms of the spiritual combat, we must
not forget how the concept of Yahweh as the Lord of Battles
seared into the consciousness of early Israel the historical
reality of its God who had revealed his name in no other
way than "watch and see." God's activity in the world is
realized on the stage of history; historical action reveals him.
Religion for ancient Israel was not a cultic communion with
the mythical time of the gods; it was as real as the waters
they had crossed, as the cities that fell before them. It was
also further confirmation of the election God had made of
them. The universalism to which the religion of Israel would
ultimately lead was never to be reached by the path of
impersonalism — a vague and general but quite impersonal
"philanthropia." When the nationalist limits of Israel would
one day be surpassed, the message of God's love would always
and ever have the inescapable element of election, personal
choice and pledge; in short, it would be a covenant-love. The
people through whom the world would be schooled to that
understanding of God reached it themselves through the this-
worldly involvement of Yahweh Sabaoth, the Lord of armies.

IV. THE PATRIARCHAL CYCLES

The stories of the Patriarchs are largely Yahwist and

Elohist traditions, joined together by genealogies of the Priestly tradition. The Elohist accounts tend to stress the transcendence of Yahweh, the "wholly other" character of his being, whereas the Yahwist stress an anthropomorphic involvement, which lays the foundation for the election of the kingdom of Judah. Both of them, of course, stress God's action in this world, the promise and the realization of land and progeny. But Abraham's faith is challenged precisely through the paradox of a promise of a this-worldly realization in the absence of any this-worldly grounds on which such a hope might rest. Thus we are introduced to the "pilgrim" dimension of the people of God: while the material object of the future hope is this-worldly, the ground of that hope is *not* a this-worldly guarantee but the very person of Yahweh Elohim — not indeed an "other-worldly" God, but rather a God who can radically create the future precisely because he is powerful and free to do so.

We are thus introduced to a theme that will run through the entire Bible: the fact that God's people may never expect to see clearly *how* the divine plan is to be realized historically; it would indeed be a weakness of Yahwistic faith if it needed successive guarantees of its ultimate achievement. In other words, if Yahwistic faith gives a concern for historical realization, it does not on the other hand become victimized by the delay of it. Faith in Yahweh schools the people to view their relation to history (this worldly realization) as Yahweh himself does: he is not so outside of history as to refuse to touch it, nor so within it as to be its victim. He is, precisely, the Lord of history. And while God's people could not pretend to have his power to make history, their faith in him gave them a confidence in the future, a sense of superiority to the ravages of time and a feeling that they were free from the shackles of fate. In stressing this conception of God, the patriarchal accounts, particularly those of Abraham, to whom all succeeding generations would look as a model of faith, give us a fresh and free conception of the world, its time and history.

2. The Creation Accounts and the Prophets

By now it is a well-accepted principle even among the non-specialists that the first three chapters of Genesis are not a blow-by-blow description of what happened scientifically in the cosmogenesis. Rather the two accounts of creation which we find in these chapters are reactions of faith by the biblical writers to the world they knew. Through a process of retrojection, they sought to give a theological explanation for man's present life-situation. Only if this is kept in mind does the full richness of the accounts appear.

Man's existence in this world, they saw, presented the paradox, just as ours does today, of sublimity and depravity, of heroism and consummate selfishness, so that one might wonder who is the more authentic commentary on man: Abel the just or his brother Cain who slew him — just as today we might ask ourselves who better represents what we are: Milton Olive, who threw himself on a grenade to save his buddies, or the anonymous murderer of Viola Liuzzo? The fact is that both represent what each of us is: the frontier between good and evil passes through the heart of each of us. The sacred writers saw this: man's moral existence is, like nature itself, a mixture of light and darkness, of night and day, and the moral chaos that threatens the dikes of human existence at every moment, and periodically breaks through, is as devastating — and as absurd — as the primeval chaos out of which the order of creation emerged.

This is at least a central theme of the creation accounts

and of the pages that follow. They are not so much interested in ascribing the being of the universe to God as they are in relating to him its order and beauty, and absolving him from any direct responsibility for the return of chaos which the sacred writers observed in the world of their day. Thus the Priestly account shows how God, whose spirit hovered over the watery abyss, by his creative word brought order and harmony to the universe: he gathered the waters, set limits to them, and made the dry land appear. The Yahwist author says the same thing in the motif of a "dry" cosmogony: into a totally desert land Yahweh brings dew and water. Land without water can be as chaotic as water without land. But at God's word or by his hand, a cosmos emerges.

It is significant that in the Yahwist account, man himself enters into and cooperates with God's work of cosmifying the world. He names the animals — and whatever man called them, *that* was their name. This is a simple detail which tells us man is not only constituted lord of the universe but that he must accept and establish his lordship by his own free acts.

This assertion by the Yahwist author about man's radical independence and freedom concerning the world around him finds a parallel in the Priestly account of creation on the fourth day, the one which describes the creation of the lights. There is a real demythologizing intent in this passage, or a "desacralizing" intent, if we wish to use that term. The peoples among whom the ancient Israelites lived thought of the stars as divine beings whose course ruled the fate of man. The sun, the moon and the constellations were worshiped. The Priestly author wishes to liberate his people from any such belief or subservience: the stars are nothing but lamps hung up in heaven by God — and he made them. And the only thing they rule is the "night" and "day" and they mark the seasons. They thus belong to the order of nature and are not makers of history. History is made by God and man alone.

Finally, the cosmifying process climaxes in the formation of the highest human unity: the oneness of marriage, which

Adam accepts, affirming woman's likeness to himself, and the two become one flesh.

The Yahwist goes on to relate the return, at least the partial return, from cosmos to chaos in terms of man's personal rebellion against the author of life and order. The primeval sin was a sin of disobedience rooted in a secretive mistrust, as the insinuation of the serpent shows (Gen 3:5). In the description of this primeval sin we are given the prototype of every sin man commits — and a magnificent psychology of its process. To borrow Paul's terms, man began to think of God no longer as being *for* him but rather as being *against* him — or at least Adam was not sure. Is God really love? Or is God just afraid man will become too independent for God's own good? The fallacy which the serpent succeeded in insinuating was the latter: namely that God is an enemy of man's freedom, of his fulfillment. This point is quite relevant to our theme, for this is precisely the image many moderns have of God — not as the author, foundation, and guarantor of man's freedom but as its enemy. Basic to this fallacy is another: a confused notion of God's transcendence. For if God must defend *himself* against the independence of man, then he is, as it were, on an equal footing with him. God is made in the image of man, as were the pagan gods of antiquity: gods who had to engage in struggle, deceit, and intrigue in order to impose their mastery.

But it is precisely against this conception of God that the sacred author is waging his polemic. The Yahwist is insisting that God's demands are not made in his own self-defense but are made in defense of man himself. The statement "man has become like one of us, with his knowledge of good and evil" (Gen 3:22) is not against this interpretation; it supports it, for the statement is ironic to the core. Man's abuse of his freedom, though inspired by a desire to know "good and evil" (an expression of the divine omniscience) ends in a knowledge of "good and evil" quite different: the experience of moral and physical chaos.

That God's claims had been made in the interest of man himself is shown in the results of the sin. For from this turning from Yahweh, the author of life, man experienced a fourfold alienation. There was first the alienation from *self*, the disintegration of his person, a sense of loss of harmony and peace — dramatized by the sense of nakedness. Man is no longer himself, and he really does not know what to do with himself except to withdraw, to escape, to flee. The second alienation man experiences is that from *others*. The "other," in this case represented by Eve, the summit of interpersonal relationships, whom Adam had praised as "flesh of his flesh, bone of his bone," now becomes Adam's scapegoat. When asked why he ate the forbidden fruit, Adam, instead of defending or excusing his wife, passes the buck to her, and even back to God: "It was the woman *you* put with me; she gave me the fruit, and I ate it" (Gen 3:12). This theme of the projection of guilt will be pursued through the first chapters of Genesis, when Cain turns on his brother Abel, kills him, and then says, "Am I my brother's guardian?" (Gen 4:10.) And Lamech's cry that he will wreak seventy-fold vengeance on anyone and kill any youth that merely bruises him simply illustrates to what social chaos man's own hands can bring him.

The third alienation is an alienation from the *order of nature*. Taken from the dust of the earth, man is linked in inevitable solidarity with it. But he is also the breath of Yahweh Elohim, and thus in man the material universe has transcended itself. Beyond that, Yahweh places him in a garden — the Babylonian royal garden, where the servant walks in the cool of day in intimacy with his king. Man was put there "to till it and to keep it." The suggestion is that, just as man shares in the cosmifying of the universe, so he will be actively responsible for maintaining this new state; yet this too will bring with it the joy of creativity. But with the fall man now finds himself in a totally savage world, illustrated by the thorns and thistles, where he must eke out his existence painfully in a long struggle against the elements. His present state is then *both* a punishment for sin and also a return to the natural state of things. Ultimately, the cosmic elements get the better of him in death, when man returns to the dust from which he was taken.

But the view of faith is that these three alienations, which can be verified in the daily experience of everyman, are rooted in a fourth, by far the most basic: man's alienation from *God*. The thought of God is no longer that of a friend with whom one walks in the cool of the evening, but of a master whom one fears and flees. The sacred author wishes to make it clear, however, that the catastrophic rupture has happened totally in man, not in God, for the very gesture of putting man out of the garden is shown to reflect God's concern that man not do himself more harm than he has already done, and God's gesture of making garments for the first pair shows his concern to shelter them from the rigors of the bitter existence they have brought on themselves.

We have seen, then, that the sacred authors of Genesis 1–3 find in the daily experience of everyman the vehicle for expressing a profound theology. We know too how the theme of progressive degeneration is pursued through the first eleven chapters: having turned against God, the author of harmony and life, man turns against his fellow man: Cain, Lamech, the marriage of the sons of God with the daughters of men — all this precipitated the flood, which is really only the return of the waters of chaos precipitated by man's sin. If in the creation account, night is the chaos of darkness driven into order and the seas and rivers are the chaos of the watery abyss driven into order, in the primitive history that follows, chaos returns in the wake of man's rebellion against the Author of life and order.[1]

It is not too early to draw from these data a conclusion

---

[1] The theme discussed here will be an important one for the prophets. It is especially striking in Hosea's stress on the knowledge of God as the foundation of social life (Hos 4:1 f; 6:14; 7:9; 9:7).

which is extremely important for the notion of redemption. If perdition is described as man's loss of his hold on his existence, as his loss of hold on life, as his decay morally and physically ending in death, then redemption will mean the restoration of man to the fullness of life and being. It will not be an escape from his bodiliness but a complete recovery of it. It will not be merely a promise that, in spite of all, there is a better life after this one is over and all we have to do is endure this vale of tears. It will rather mean the return to life here and now, the healing of man's alienations, the reintegration of his life in every dimension.

Perhaps I can illustrate this by an example, of which you could doubtless give me parallels from your own experience. One Sunday afternoon I was walking across our campus in San Antonio. It is a rather dead place on Sunday afternoons, since everyone is either at a ball game, on a date, or just out somewhere enjoying the good old Texas sun. Consequently when I spotted a student standing alone about ten feet from the science building and just staring at it, I immediately suspected something was wrong. He was obviously absorbed in his thoughts, as he did not see or hear me approaching. When I said hello, he turned quickly at me in surprise. I could tell from the expression on his face that he was in a pretty bad emotional state. With a few vague lead questions on my part, he began pouring out his troubles, and we began walking slowly toward my office. It was a sort of typical pattern. Loosed from the freedom of home, he had done just about everything, and now the end of the semester was approaching and everything was closing in on him. His health was beginning to suffer too — lack of sleep and appetite. He had all but given up his faith (the old cliché "I don't want to be a hypocrite"). Here is an example where the flight from reality and from life showed up in every dimension of his being — not only the spiritual and moral, but the emotional and even the physical. Recovery for this young man would mean a recovery of life, light, reality, and order in every dimension in which he had experienced disorder. Redemption would mean the healing of the various alienations he had driven himself to: from God, from others, and from the world in which he no longer found reason for existing.

What is true in this example is true today on a world-scale: whatever activity is aimed at healing man as man or reconciling man with man can be and already is redemptive, even if only partially so. At any rate, a message of redemption which is unwilling to incorporate all human healing and reconciling activity will, by the verdict of the Bible itself, condemn itself to irrelevance. The great opportunity today is precisely that the world is open to and looking for a mystique which will unite and impel all these forces for good. We shall return to this thought later, because it is picked up again in the New Testament.

II. THE PROPHETS

Although there were some remarkable forerunners, the prophetic movement in Israel is really associated with the settled life and with the problems it raised. The prophets are rightly associated, in popular thought even today, with the promise of the Messiah — but their role of foretelling the future was only subsidiary. It emerged only out of other more direct preoccupations. And those direct preoccupations were to deliver God's judgment upon the contemporary scene of Israel's religion and politics. It is a complete misconception of Israelite prophetism to imagine the prophet sitting in a hermitage dreaming about some mythical future and then uttering an oracle about the utopia to come. No, the prophets were men intensely wrapped up in the public life of the day, the life of the court, the sanctuary, the city gate. And their turning to the future was something that they were forced to by the contemporary deterioration of events. It is important to note that the political life of Israel is the area of God's concern, and the future hope emerges from and is always related to the this-worldly scene.

By the same token, the prophets hasten Israel's "coming of age" by a ruthless process of relativizing the three most important institutions in Israel: kingship, liturgy, and even prophetism. I have used the term "relativization" where others have used the term "desacralization," because I do not think the latter is etymologically an exact term for the process. It suggests that the prophets were out to strip king, priest, and prophet of all holiness, and this is simply not so. That holiness was, however, a relative thing: rather than making the office-holder invulnerable to criticism, it was rather a challenge to his personal integrity to live up to the exalted role he was called to fulfill among God's people.

Kingship

The institution of kingship was not adopted without great hesitation, and it is likely that the prophet Samuel was himself divided by the reasons for and against. God alone was king; was there not a danger that a king for Israel would threaten the very roots of Yahwism? The danger was very real, but thanks to succeeding generations of prophets, the relative character of the king in Israel was never lost from view. We see this in Nathan's criticism of David for his adultery and murder (2 Sam 12). There are two things to note about this account: (1) The king is not absolute; he is not God; he is subject to divine judgment and to covenant law as much as any commoner; (2) the heinousness of David's crime is increased by the holiness of the office he bears. "Nathan said to David: 'You are the man. Yahweh the God of Israel says this, "I anointed you king over Israel. . . . Why have you shown contempt for Yahweh, doing what displeases him?" ' " (1 Sam 12:7–9). The religious character of the office increases the gravity of the crime. This is worth pointing out to those who speak of total secularization as having its roots in the Bible. If secularization means that politics is to be politics and not some divine order immune to criticism, yes. But to say that there was a divorce of religion from secular life is not a sufficiently *radical* view of the situation. Religion is not a whitewash of a political institution; but neither is it indifferent to it, or divorced from it. *Religion sits in judgment on politics.* It brings to politics an added motivation for doing its job well. This is why I prefer the term "relativization" of politics rather than "desacralization."

The prophetic literature is filled with examples of the prophets criticizing kings: from Elijah's condemnation of Ahab in the Naboth incident (1 Kgs 21) to Jeremiah's blistering Philippic on Jehoiakim (Jer 22:13–19):

> Doom for the man who founds his palace on anything but integrity, his upstairs rooms on anything but honesty, who makes his fellow man work for nothing, without paying him his wages. . . .

The theology behind this stand is given in Jeremiah 21:11–22:9: The Davidic monarchy has the obligation under God of establishing justice in society, specifically of defending the rights of the helpless as demanded in covenant law (e.g., Ex 22:20–23). If it discharges this obligation, its existence is justified and it will endure; but since this is not so, it is under judgment.

Worship

While modern scholarship is retreating from the position popular some years ago to the effect that the prophets were anti-cultic *per se*, it is nonetheless true that they more than any other factor contributed to the spiritualization of worship, to directing it toward another end, in other words, to de-absolutizing it. Against the complacency at Bethel, Amos shouts out:

> I hate and despise your feasts,
> I take no pleasure in your solemn festivals.
> When you offer me holocausts,
> I reject your oblations,

and refuse to look at your sacrifices of fattened cattle.
Let me have no more of the din of your chanting,
no more of your strumming on harps.
But let justice flow like water,
and integrity like an unfailing stream (5:21–24).

At the other end of the pre-exilic spectrum, Jeremiah waged the same battle against the complacency of Jerusalem. The prevailing belief was that God would not, indeed could not, allow the city and the temple to be destroyed. The inviolability of Zion had become a religious principle, a means of avoiding covenant obligations, and practically of defying Yahweh to punish the people. Religion had really become the opium of the people, and it was Jeremiah's sad task in the name of Yahweh to protest this complacency.

The word that was addressed to Jeremiah by Yahweh, "Go and stand at the gate of the Temple of Yahweh and there proclaim this message. Say, 'Listen to the word of Yahweh, all you men of Judah who come in by these gates to worship Yahweh. Yahweh Sabaoth, the God of Israel, says this: Amend your behaviour and your actions and I will stay with you here in this place. Put no trust in delusive words like these: This is the sanctuary of Yahweh, the sanctuary of Yahweh, the sanctuary of Yahweh! But if you do amend your behaviour and your actions, if you treat each other fairly, if you do not exploit the stranger, the orphan and the widow (if you do not shed innocent blood in this place), and if you do not follow alien gods, to your own ruin, then here in this place I will stay with you, in the land that long ago I gave to your fathers for ever. Yet here you are, trusting in delusive words, to no purpose! Steal, would you, murder, commit adultery, perjure yourselves, burn incense to Baal, follow alien gods that you do not know? and then come presenting yourselves in this Temple that bears my name, saying: Now we are safe — safe to go on committing all these abominations! Do you take this Temple that bears my name for a robbers' den? I, at any rate, am not blind — it is Yahweh who speaks' " (Jer 7:1–11).

It is the temptation of religion of all ages to divorce itself from daily life, to provide a comfortable retreat from the world. The prophets of ancient Israel left a lasting monument to the fact that true worship is that which brings one closer to the reality of life, not farther away from it.

Prophetism

In the ancient Near East, prophetism was a profession. It certainly was not confined to Israel; and in Israel itself, there were bands of prophets who made a living from their oracles. It must not have been easy to recognize the voice of a true prophet amid the many voices claiming to speak in Yahweh's name. It was perhaps for this reason that when Amos, the shepherd from Tekoa, came to Bethel to preach, he said, "I was no prophet, neither did I belong to any of the brotherhoods of prophets. . . . I was a shepherd and looked after sycamores but it was Yahweh who took me from holding the flock, and Yahweh who said, 'Go, prophesy to my people Israel' " (Am 7:14–16). The prophetic office is not an absolute either. Amos wanted to dissociate himself completely from those "professionals" who may be quite skilled in the methods of visions and esoteric mysteries. He wants the word of God to come directly to the people afresh, uncluttered by the image of the institution.

Likewise, the classical prophets of Israel show a distinct preference for revelation by *word* rather than by dream, delirium, or even vision. Already in Elijah we see this process at work. When Elijah fled to Mount Horeb, where Yahweh had first revealed himself in the storm and fire theophany,

> Then the word of Yahweh came to him saying . . . "Go out and stand on the mountain before Yahweh." Then Yahweh himself went by. There came a mighty wind, so strong it tore the mountains and shattered the rocks before Yahweh. But Yahweh was not in the wind. After the wind came an earthquake. But Yahweh was not in the earthquake. And after the earthquake came a fire. But Yahweh was not in the fire. And after the fire there came the sound of a gentle breeze[2] . . . (1 Kgs 19:9, 11–13).

---

[2] The "gentle breeze," of the Jerusalem Bible is more familiar to English readers as "a still, small voice." No matter what the translation, the point is basically the same, namely, a down-playing of extraordinary phenomena and a support of the more tranquil forms of divine revelation. Cf. J. Lindblom, *Prophecy in Ancient Israel* (Philadelphia: Fortress Press, 1965), p. 48. I am indebted to Dr. Lou H. Silberman of Vanderbilt University for

The same emphasis on revelation by spoken word rather than vision is found in Jeremiah 1:4–10 and Isaiah 40:1 ff.

Thus we can say that the prophets purified even the institution of prophetism; they helped to humanize it, or to "demythologize" it. They turned the attention of the people to the critical importance of daily life in religion. Now let us turn to their contribution to the future hope. We said earlier that the prophets' leap to the future was occasioned by the failure of the kings to live up to the covenant and to apply it to the land. God would one day achieve the promise of the covenant, even if the incumbent king abdicated his responsibilities. Isaiah 7, 9, and 11 develop this hope: God will achieve his plan despite Ahaz' infidelity; the Queen-Mother will have a son in whom the ideal will be achieved. But not even with Hezekiah was the kingdom of peace achieved, and Isaiah in his later oracles probably did not even expect it any longer in his own lifetime.

Now one might be led to think that this wistful turning to the future might simply be a retreat and acceptance of failure in this-worldly activity. In one sense it was: it was the admission that we do not have yet the kingdom of God. But this "eschatological anguish," if I may so put it, far from halting the concern for change, rather spurred it on. It was precisely the smug, the complacent defenders of the status quo, those who lacked the sense of the covenant, whose very this-worldly activity ceased to lead anywhere. The prophet became the witness to eschatology. And the question he asks today, as then, is not, "Are you in the world?" but "what are you *doing* there?"

No one typifies this eschatological witness better than Jeremiah. He stood alone against the city, its leaders and its "prophets," proclaiming the inevitable destruction of Jerusalem because no one was paying heed to the covenant. Jere-

---

pointing out to me that the very choice of vocabulary in the Mount Horeb incident indicates a polemic against what the author feels is an excessively externalized theophany in Exodus 19.

miah's celibacy was part of this prophetic and eschatological witness. It pointed to the end. When the end did come and Jerusalem was leveled and the temple looted and razed, when all the feverish this-worldly stratagems were wiped clean out of existence, the seed of rebirth lay under the ashes. It had been planted by Jeremiah. But for him, Israel might never have recovered.

The history of Israel and her prophets shows, then, that a total secularization of life is not the answer. Somewhere there must be a witness who stands apart and brings to political and social life the judgment of a different order. This will be the prophetic role of the Church. If she abdicates it, it will not only be the Church that suffers; it will be the world.

The Exile

The Exile was the crucible of purification. It schooled the remnant in at least three ways: (1) The mobility of Yahweh was reaffirmed. During the desert wanderings, Yahweh had gone with his people wherever they went; but by Jeremiah's time, his residence had come to be viewed as so stably fixed to the temple of Jerusalem as to overshadow and obscure the spiritual indwelling which it was meant to represent. Ezekiel assured the people that God's glory had left Jerusalem and had come to dwell with his people in exile (Ez 10), where he was their only sanctuary (Ez 11:15). (2) Yet the spiritualization was not a complete abandoning of the temporal realization; it was linked to the hope of restoration (cf. Ez 11:15 ff.). (3) The contact with pagan tribes and new pagan mythologies led to a greater universalism in Israel's religion.

The prophet who distilled the essence of the new insights was the anonymous "Second Isaiah," who wrote toward the end of the exile. He is a prophet of the good news, the messenger of consolation, the herald of the return.

Second Isaiah describes the return as a New Exodus. Thus

in Chapter 43, it is the Exodus he is evoking when, of the
return, he has God say, "Do not be afraid, for I have redeemed you; I have called you by your name, you are mine
(Covenant motif). Should you pass through the sea, I will
be with you; or through rivers, they will not swallow you up"
(43:1–2). Or again: "With one threat I can dry up the sea
and turn rivers to desert; so that their fish shrivel up for
want of water and die of thirst" (50:2). This "double
exposure" technique explains the curious juxtaposition of the
following verses:

> I am he who . . . confirms the word of my servant and makes
> the plans of my envoys succeed. I am he who says of Jerusalem,
> "Let her be inhabited," of the towns of Judah, "Let them be
> rebuilt," and I will raise their ruins once more. I am he who
> says to the ocean, "Be dry. I will dry up your rivers" (Is
> 44:26–27).

Finally, in 51:9–11 we read:

> Awake, awake! Clothe yourself in strength,
> arm of Yahweh.
> Awake, as in the past,
> in times of generations long ago.
> Did you not split Rahab in two,
> and pierce the Dragon through?
> Did you not dry up the sea,
> the waters of the great Abyss,
> to make the seabed a road
> for the redeemed to cross?
> Those whom Yahweh has ransomed return,
> they come to Zion shouting for joy,
> everlasting joy in their faces;
> joy and gladness go with them,
> sorrow and lament are ended.

However, the return will not be *merely* a return of the
Exodus. It will have a newness all its own:

> Thus says Yahweh
> who made a way through the sea,
> a path in the great waters;
> who put chariots and horse in the field
> and a powerful army,
> which lay there never to rise again,

> snuffed out, put out like a wick:
> No need to recall the past,
> no need to think about what was done before.
> See, I am doing a new deed,
> even now it comes to light; can you not see it?
> Yes, I am making a road in the wilderness,
> paths in the wilds . . . (Is 43:16–19).

Thus the new event is more than a cultic return of a past event; it is the projecting forward of God's people in history; this is why the event is described not only as a new Exodus but also as a New Creation.

It is principally to Second Isaiah that we owe the Bible's theology of creation. Because the Priestly account of creation occupies the first page of the Bible and obviously describes what took place first in time, it has been the natural tendency to conclude that this account represents the earliest theological insight of the Bible. This is not so. The Priestly account, in its present form at least, dates from the exile, and it is dependent on, or at least closely related to Second Isaiah.[3] Let us see how this theology evolved.

Israel was very slow, even reluctant, to admit speculation about creation into her sacred traditions. The pagan creation myths and nature cycles seemed not only pagan but really irrelevant to a nation committed to an ongoing, historical future. That Yahweh had control over the forces of nature was, of course, understood from the time of the Exodus onward, but it was precisely through historical events that Israel came to this conviction — e.g., the victory Song of Deborah depicts Yahweh commanding the stars to fight against Sisera (Jgs 5:20).

By the time Second Isaiah wrote, however, another important factor in Israel's historical evolution had become seared on the conscience of the people: the power of the *prophetic* word. Already Amos and Hosea had extolled the power of God's word: "I slaughtered them with the words

---

[3] Cf. John L. McKenzie, *Myths and Realities* (Milwaukee: The Bruce Publishing Company, 1963), p. 53 f.

from my mouth" (Hos 6:5). And Jeremiah: "Does not my word burn like fire . . . is it not like a hammer shattering a rock?" (Jer 23:29.) Jeremiah's words were not listened to — until the catastrophe of 588–587 B.C. proved his word to have indeed been Yahweh's — or, as Yahweh says to Ezekiel: "As far as they (my people) are concerned . . . you are like a love song beautifully sung to music. They listen to your words, but no one puts them into practice. When the thing takes place — and it is beginning now — they will learn that there has been a prophet among them" (Ez 33:32–33).

But return and restoration after the exile had also been promised by the prophets. Second Isaiah witnessed the fulfillment of this promise, the truth of the divine word:

> Things now past I once revealed long ago,
> they went out from my mouth and I proclaimed them;
> then suddenly I acted and they happened (Is 48:3).

Thus, as the return loomed on the horizon, the exiles found a new conviction of the power of the prophetic word. From this, Israel came to see God's word as possessing creative power that was not only historical but cosmic. How did this happen?

The exiles lived amid a people mesmerized by the pantheon of nature gods, the recital of the *Enuma elish,* and the elaborate liturgy of *akitu,* the Babylonian New Year Feast. Each year the exiles would witness the grandiose procession of Marduk down the sacred way of Babylon, flanked by the lions of Ishtar. The monsters Marduk had conquered in his cosmic battle followed in his cortege. The feast celebrated his victory over Tiamat and the primeval chaos. The other gods, with their solar emblems, were borne about on chariots. Marduk on this feast recreated the world and renewed its fertility; and even the divine world of the constellations was remade. The stars were the figures of the beasts and monsters of the *Enuma elish,* with names we recognize today: Hydra, Leo, Capricorn, Sagittarius, Aquarius. And of course, the destinies of men were ruled by the stars.

The fall of Babylon and the return of the exiles was Yahweh's victory over the gods Babylon had venerated as cosmic creators. The idols had effectively been reduced to "wind and waste" (*tohu,* the primeval chaos, Is 41:29). What this great event proved for the faith of Israel was that "toward the rising and the setting of the sun men may know that there is none besides me. I am the Lord, there is no other" (Is 45:6). Everything, including chaos, is in Yahweh's power: "I form the light, and create the darkness, I make well-being and create woe; I, Yahweh, do all these things" (Is 45:7).

This is why the victory over Babylon shows that God is Lord and creator of the stars. Second Isaiah makes Babylon's sorcery and star-worship the point of his taunt to the collapsing city:

> Keep to your spells then,
> and all your sorceries,
> for which you have worn yourself out since your youth.
> Do you think they will help you?
> Do you think they will make anyone nervous?
> You have spent weary hours with your many advisers,
> Let them come forward now
> and save you, these who analyze the heavens,
> who study the stars
> and announce month by month
> what will happen to you next.

> Oh, they will be like wisps of straw
> and the fire will burn them.
> They will not save their lives
> from the power of the flame.
> No embers these, for baking,
> no fireside to sit by.
> This is what your wizards will be for you,
> those men for whom you have worn yourself out since your youth.
> They will all go off, each his own way,
> powerless to save you (Is 47:12–15).

From this it was easy to see that the stars are not forces that determine man's destiny; they are merely lamps for the universe, serving to mark the changes of the season (Gen 1:14–15). They are, moreover, God's creatures. There is a truly liberating breath in Genesis' short statement: *"And he made the stars*" (Gen 1:16). Second Isaiah says it poetically: "Lift up your eyes on high and see who has created these: he leads out their army and numbers them, calling them all by name" (40:26). The point worth underlining is that the cosmic power of Yahweh is nothing but an *extension* of his loving care for his people, and Israel is brought to understand his cosmic omnipotence precisely by the same kind of process that she had learned anything else about Yahweh: through a concrete event on the plane of historical action.

This is borne out by the usage Second Isaiah makes of *bārā', to create*. The word is used only of action by Yahweh; its first usage is of the deeds that Yahweh and he alone does for his people, "*making* history" (e.g., Ex 34:10 — making the covenant and working historical marvels for his people). Second Isaiah continues this usage — in fact it is the primary sense in which he uses it (Is 43:14; 45:8) — but extending it now to the cosmic creation and to the creation of man: "Yahweh is the eternal God, *creator* of the ends of the earth" (Is 40:28); "I myself made the earth, and man upon it is my *creature (barati)*" (45:12).

Accompanying this extension of the meaning of *bārā'* is the motif of God's creation by his *word* — which prepares Genesis 1. As God's prophetic word had given existence to historical events, so his creative word gives existence to the material universe. For God, to call is to create, whether this be the creation of Israel (Is 43:1) or the creation of the universe (Is 40:26).

Applied now to the universe, the idea of God's creation by his word is still charged with all the personalism it had for historical creation. The creation of the universe, proceeding from God's word, according to his plan (Is 55:11), expresses the same loving design, the same personal gift and call, as his saving acts in time and history. In fact, it is the first of his saving acts — what the Priestly author will list as the *first* of his "generations" (Gen 2:4a).

Thus Israel came to the notion of cosmic creation through her experience of historical creation: the newness of her experience of Yahweh, who is never bound to a cycle and not even merely to reproduce his own deeds of the past, makes possible the dawning of the realization that the very material universe had in a similar fashion *come to be*. This is why, too, the thought of a new creation is also used to describe the age to come, the future yet to be made — why the future is essentially open-ended and undetermined, because it too, like the depths of the sea, is held in the hollow of his hand (cf. Is 40:12).

3. The Synoptic Gospels: The Kingdom of God

This chapter will examine the theology of the secular in the synoptics. Since a selection among the possible approaches imposes itself, it seems best to choose the most central motif of the synoptics, that of the "kingdom of God." At least this theme appears chiefly in the synoptics and was the favorite subject of Jesus' preaching. If anything can help us toward a theology of the secular, it should be this theme. We must first, however, bridge the gap from the Restoration to New Testament times.

1. THE RISE OF APOCALYPTIC AND KINGDOM OF GOD THEME

In post-exilic times the formation of the Bible is characterized by two important developments: the rise of the problem literature and the appearance of apocalyptic.

Since we have to make a choice amid the vast material of the Old Testament, we shall limit our observations on the Wisdom literature to the consideration that much of it, the problem literature at least, challenged the old Deuteronomic theology concerning reward in this world for observance of the Torah. Experience shows, the authors of the problem literature said, that this does not always work out in practice — in fact, with such frequency does the just man suffer that the principle of an infallible reward here and now can really be proven bankrupt. The Wisdom literature thus helped purify the motivation for observing the Covenant, and it helped to thrust the Covenant relationship beyond death (cf. Wis 1:15; Ps 16:10; 73:23–26).

The problem that made the Sages agonize over the theology of God's justice to the individual also gave rise to another kind of literature which grappled with the problem of that same justice on the national and international levels: apocalyptic. Like the problem literature, it arose from an attempt to reconcile faith in God's sovereign command of world events, on the one hand, and the obvious facts of experience on the other — particularly the experience of persecution and martyrdom such as occurred under Antiochus IV Epiphanes.

It is important to understand what a major crisis of faith Israel underwent at this time. The apocalyptists, and other pious Jews of the time, did not want a pagan sword to wipe out a conception of God which it had taken centuries to achieve — namely of God as universal ruler of cosmos and history. At the risk of repeating some ideas brought out in previous chapters, let us recall something of the price that had been paid, historically, for this achievement.

In spite of the purer notion of God implied in the name Yahweh (i.e., God's radical independence and freedom from any magical invocation), in spite of the covenant as an expression primarily of God's sovereign demands upon his people (and not the people's control of God), Israel had a hard time freeing herself of the conception of a "God in a box," and even the voice of Jeremiah failed to do so, until the fall of Jerusalem proved him true.

For the most part, in the early days, most Israelites shared the common belief that their God was a territorial god, limited to the boundaries and the subjects who worshiped him (cf. Chemosh over Moab and Milcom over Ammon, 1 Kgs 11:33). The account of Naaman the Syrian transporting dirt from Israel into the territory of Rimmon (2 Kgs 5:17–18) reflects the conception that land was as essential to Yahweh as Yahweh was important to the land. For Yahweh to give up his land would be to disinherit himself. Thus Yahweh was

thought of as possessing that most basic of human drives —
to own and defend territory.[1]

Along with this crude conception was the other *functional*
conception that Yahweh, like the gods of the pagan tribes,
was a god whose main job was to provide help in time of
war, counsel through soothsayers or sages, or judgment in
cases of justice too hard for human decision.

We have seen how the prophets attacked these misconcep-
tions, particularly the thought that God is nothing but a
helper in time of need. While not denying this point, the
prophets insisted that God is God and has his own demands
on his people, a God of justice and the defender of the
oppressed. His justice extends to all nations, and Israel will
be punished for her crimes as much as will any other nation
(Am 1–2). By the same token, the deeds of all nations fall
into his plan and under his control: it was not a foreign god
but Yahweh himself who brought the Philistines from Caphtor
and the Syrians from Kir (Am 9:7; cf. Is 5:26; Jer 27:5–11).

The experience of the exile, however, presented an addi-
tional challenge to this faith by pointing up a seemingly final
dilemma to which the "our God" theology on the one hand,
and the ever-brighter monotheism, on the other, led. On the
one hand, Yahweh is King of Israel; on the other, he is the
only God, standing for universal justice, and his kingship
extends over the whole earth. Now, if the people who worshiped Yahweh became subject to the "unjust" who worshiped other gods, does this not mean that Yahweh himself
is subject to these other gods? The prophets of the exile had
spoken of the *Day of the Lord*. The inevitable intervention of
God, if not visible now, will come on that day — a day of
judgment but also the day, as later prophets saw, that would
usher in the rule of God, his direct reign over all men, a kind
of golden age (Is 2:2–4; 11:6–9; Mic 4:1–4).

It was this traditional conception which the apocalyptists

---

[1] Here it is instructive to read Robert Ardrey's recent work, *Territorial
Imperative* (New York: Athenaum, 1966).

seized on to resolve the antinomy between Israel's faith in the absolute power and sovereignty of Yahweh and the facts of experience. They developed it in the conception of the *reign of God* or the *kingdom of God* — a conception central to understanding the message of the synoptics.

Obviously, it referred to something in the future. The rule of God was to usher in the "Age to Come," which was to be quite different from the present age. Man's existence in this future age was called by the Rabbis "the life of the Age to Come," of which an equivalent is "eternal life." These expressions are far more frequent in the Rabbinic literature than "Kingdom of God," with which they are identical.

Besides this futuristic conception, there is a certain qualified dualism in the Apocalyptic literature: God's work is countered by an adversary, Satan. We say qualified because, while Satan leads the forces of evil in this world and sometimes seems to be winning, his action is only permitted by God, and he and all evil will ultimately be overthrown in a cosmic battle.

The Apocalypses diverge in their descriptions of how this kingdom is to come about. Some of them speak about the establishment of the kingdom without mention of any mediator (e.g., *Assumption of Moses* 10:1). At other times some kind of mediator is mentioned — the Messiah (*Apocalypse of Baruch* 73) or the Son of Man (Dan 7:14, developed in *Henoch* especially).

The Rabbis had their own way of using this eschatological hope to turn the people's attention to the Torah, which was for them the supreme vehicle of God's relations with men. For them God's rule is something one accepts by submitting to God's will in the Torah. This happened to Israel as a nation on Mount Sinai in accepting the covenant. The proselyte in his turn by accepting the Torah "takes upon himself the kingdom of heaven," an action repeated each time the Jew himself recites the daily Shema (Deut 6:4–5). This interpretation, which was more demythologized, did not become normative for Judaism until after the emergence of Christianity.

In the first century, then, the hope for the immediate in-breaking of God's rule was such a commonplace that the prayer of the Kaddish, which pious Jews recited then just as they do today, concluded with the request: "May he establish his kingdom during your life and during your days, and during the life of all the house of Israel."

II. The Preaching by John the Baptist

This explains no doubt why the preaching of John the Baptist and of Jesus himself found willing ears when both approached their message via the "kingdom of God" motif. According to Matthew 3:2, John's message was essentially what Jesus' would be when he opened his ministry, "Repent, for the kingdom of heaven is close at hand." John, then, preached the imminence of God's reign, his intervention. Significantly, however, the God who intervenes is depicted not as a victorious and bellicose king but rather as a divine judge coming to set everything aright. The day of his coming will be one of wrath and fire (Mt 3:12) — prophetic motifs calculated to win the people to a true moral conversion.

III. Jesus and the Kingdom of God

When Jesus began his ministry, then, not only was the "kingdom of God" theme a living preoccupation among the people; its relation to a moral renewal had at least been aired by John the Baptist. Now the hills of Galilee began to ring with a new voice, a voice at once disturbing and consoling. It announced God's kingdom and laid down its severe demands. The voice was that of Jesus of Nazareth.

Controversy has raged among the Scripture scholars as to whether Jesus preached the kingdom of God as coming or as already present. The major trend today is to admit that both elements are present in his message.

A. *The Kingdom as Coming and Imminent*

We have seen that the Jews of the early first century felt that the kingdom of God had not yet arrived but was coming soon. It is certain that Jesus picked up this element and used it in his preaching. Mark 1:15 is the most prominent example: "The time has come . . . and the kingdom of God is close at hand. Repent, and believe the Good News."[2] It is the same message he gives to his disciples in sending them forth to preach (Mt 10:7; Lk 10:9, 11). He foretells that some of those listening to him will see the kingdom be realized (Mk 9:1; Mt 16:28).

How does Jesus *use* the futuristic and imminent dimension of the kingdom in his preaching? He uses it first to describe the future condition of the elect. In Mark 9:43–47; 10:17, 24, 25 the term "Kingdom of God" is used alternately with "life" and "eternal life." The latter term, as we saw above, was the normal rabbinic expression for the condition of the elect in the future life. In this future condition, the elect will be "like angels" (Mk 12:45). But who are the elect? They are those who have accepted God's call to the kingdom in the preaching of Jesus (Mk 10:15; Mt 11:25; Lk 10:21).

Jesus likewise uses the future or eschatological meaning to explain the significance of the Last Supper. It is an anticipation, a kind of sacrament of the Messianic banquet which will characterize the kingdom of God (Mt 8:11; cf. Lk 13:28–29). It is at the Passover meal itself that Jesus says: "And now I confer a kingdom on you, just as my Father conferred one on me: you wll eat and drink at my table in my kingdom" (Lk 22:29–30). And because the meal is also an anticipation of his death, it is clear that Jesus used the concept of the coming kingdom to teach his disciples once more what he had often told them before: that his death is a necessary prelude to the coming of the kingdom. It will

---

[2] The translation *at hand* is the most convincing, in spite of the attempt of Dodd (*The Parables of the Kingdom,* pp. 29 f.) and others to translate it as "is here."

be the same message he gives at his trial: "You will see the Son of Man seated at the right hand of the Power and coming with the clouds of heaven" (Mk 14:62).

But Jesus also uses the thought of the imminence of the kingdom to urge preparation for the impending crisis. We see this in the parable of the wise and foolish maidens (Mt 25:1–13); the parable of the talents in Mt 25:14–30, which in Luke's version (Lk 19:11–27) was told to those who "imagined that the kingdom of God was going to show itself then and there" (Lk 19:11); the thief in the night (Mt 24:43–44; Lk 12:39–40); the faithful and unfaithful servants (Mt 24:45–51; Lk 12:42–46); the servants of the absent master (Mk 13:33–37). Even more graphically does the kingdom theme become functional in the description of the final judgment: Those who hear the sentence, "Enter the kingdom" are those who have practiced real love for those about them in need.

Finally, in the prayer that Jesus teaches his disciples the yearning for the coming of God's kingdom is clearly one of the attitudes Jesus expects his disciples to have: "Thy kingdom come!" As a matter of fact, in Matthew's version, each of the petitions is capable of an eschatological interpretation: may the time come when God's name is hallowed everywhere, when his will is manifest and done by all. Give us *today* the bread that is to come tomorrow (*ep-iousion*) — i.e., introduce us to the messianic banquet. Spare us from the great eschatological trial (*perasmos*) and free us in the final encounter with the Evil one (Satan).[3]

It is obvious from all these instances that Jesus uses the future dimension of the kingdom to focus attention on the critical importance of man's here-and-now response. The kingdom as future is real but functional. It teaches us to repent, convert, and accept the call to the kingdom which

---

[3] Cf. R. E. Brown's essay, "The *Pater Noster* as an Eschatological Prayer" in *New Testament Essays* (Milwaukee: Bruce IMPACT Books, 1965).

Jesus gives; to watch — i.e., to live constantly in the light of the final judgment, particularly by charity, and to pray.

B. *The Kingdom as Present*

Already in his functional, prophetic use of the coming-kingdom theme Jesus has stripped the popular conception of many of its magical, automatic, escapist traits. The coming judgment fires to change of conduct and to action here and now. But we can say more than that. For all that really is crucial, the kingdom is present and available here and now.

This is shown, first of all, in the constant synoptic theme of Jesus' exorcising the devil. The actions of Jesus and their repeated use in the synoptic material have a definite apologetic aim, and Jesus is the first to point it out: "But if it is through the finger of God that I cast out devils, then know that the kingdom of God *has overtaken* you" (Lk 11:20; cf. Mt 12:28). The kingdom has appeared, it is here, God's reign has begun. This conclusion is implied in another of Jesus' sayings: "How can anyone make his way into a strong man's house and burgle his property, unless he has tied up the strong man first? Only then can he burgle his house" (Mt 12:29 par). The "strong man," discussed here in the context of exorcism, is certainly Satan; and the belief was common that in the final age Satan would be bound. If Jesus has bound Satan and is moreover plundering his house, then the final times have begun.

God has not awaited the repentance of man to begin his kingdom. Rather it is a great manifestation of his mercy that to an unrepentant generation he should already give signs of the beginning of that kingdom — to provoke his people to repentance. The *Testament of Dan* (5:31–6:4) had said, "On the day when Israel is converted, the kingdom of the Enemy will be brought to an end." But Jesus is saying that his exorcisms show that God has not waited for repentance, that in Jesus God has already breached the walls of Satan's kingdom — and you'd better get on the winning side!

The miracles of Jesus, particularly the cures of disease, blindness, and lameness, witness to the same fact. If we picture the "kingdom of this world" as the synoptics do, we must imagine an ancient city dominated by a fortified acropolis. Satan and sin rule from the acropolis; they reign over mankind in tyranny. The outer walls of the defenses, which are the first to meet the eye, are disease, suffering, and death; they are the external witnesses to the more profound grip of sin which lies upon man. Jesus' curing of disease, healing the sick, comforting the suffering and raising the dead mean that in him God has made the crucial and definitive breach in those walls, just as the exorcisms show that already Satan is being bound.

Indeed, Jesus himself declares that history is divided into two epochs: that of the reign of the Law and the Prophets, and that of the kingdom of God. John the Baptist is the watershed between the two (Mt 11:12–13 = Lk 16:16; Mk 12:41–42 = Lk 11:31–32).

But the saying of Jesus which is most pointed toward present realization is that of Luke 7:20–21:

> Asked by the Pharisees when the kingdom of God was to come, he gave them this answer, "The coming of the kingdom of God does not admit of observation and there will be no one to say, 'Look here! Look there!' For, you must know, the kingdom of God is among you."

The alternative translation, "within you," is also possible. Whichever is chosen, Jesus is underlining the present nature of the kingdom. He is truly here demythologizing the popular conception of a sudden spectacular intervention on God's part for which no other preparation was needed by man than a complacent passivity.

The parables of growth work in the same direction. Of the many (Mt 13:24; Lk 13:18–19; Lk 13:20–21) one will suffice: that proper to Mark, the seed that grows silently:

> He also said, "This is what the kingdom of God is like. A man throws seed on the land. Night and day, while he sleeps, when

he is awake, the seed is sprouting and growing; how, he does not know. Of its own accord the land produces first the shoot, then the ear, then the full grain in the ear. And when the crop is ready, he loses no time: he starts to reap because the harvest has come" (Mk 4:26–29).

What is most important to realize is that this is how Jesus describes the *kingdom of God!* He is surely reacting against a false popular conception. The inbreaking of God's kingdom was thought to be spectacular; no, it comes as humbly as a grain of wheat falling on the sod. The kingdom was to come suddenly; no, Jesus says, it comes slowly, progressively. The kingdom was coming but not yet here; no, Jesus says, it is present already in its seed and its sprout — in Jesus and his preaching.

We can see the same demythologizing intent in the temptation accounts. From the very beginning of his ministry Jesus rejects three false but widespread Messianic ideals: to provide an economic paradise miraculously ("Not by bread alone"); to be a magician winning attention by marvelous feats totally unrelated to human needs (jumping off the pinnacle of the temple); and finally, to establish a worldwide political kingdom without God.

This evidence suffices to show how Jesus accepted the concept of the kingdom of God as a starting point. How could he have spoken meaningfully to his contemporaries if he had not? But he so re-defined it, so re-oriented it, so thrust it beyond the popular conceptions of the apocalypses, that it really was an entirely new content that he gave it. The kingdom of God is not a cataclysmic event miraculously transforming the earth and ushering in an "age to come" so incomparably different from the "present age" as to nullify any attempt to see it presently begun. Quite the contrary, with Jesus the forces of the "age to come" have invaded the present age and are already at work. The kingdom has really begun, it is here. Although it promises a consummation still to come, it is above all related to a renewed moral life right now derived from a better understanding of who God is: the Father whom Jesus reveals. It has its discipline: for it everything else must be sacrificed (Mt 6:33; Lk 12:31; the parables of the treasure and the pearl, Mt 13:44–46; no sacrifice is too great, Mk 9:43–47). It demands detachment and totally committed service (Lk 9:61–62). Its program is given in the Sermon on the Mount (Mt 5–7).

The kingdom is likewise related to the community of Jesus' disciples here and now, the little flock (Lk 12:32) to whom the kingdom will be given. But Jesus' words also urge a realistic view of this community — it will have many imperfections which must be lived with before the final harvest (Mt 13:24–30, 36–43, 47–50). Hence, Jesus interprets the kingdom of God in terms meaningful to the very real existence of his hearers.

The most significant area of "demythologizing" the kingdom appears, however, in the relationship of suffering to the kingdom and its coming. The idea of suffering as a necessary pre-condition for the coming of the Messiah or the kingdom was well accepted in Judaism. The lessons of the prophets, particularly the example of Jeremiah, and the purgatorial lesson of the exile were too vivid in the tradition of Israel to be quickly erased. Thus Jewish tradition spoke then and since of the "birth pangs" of the Messiah, namely the suffering that some, if not all, the people would have to endure to merit the coming of the Messiah. In the apocalyptic work called *The Assumption of Moses,* the composition of which R. H. Charles dates to the years A.D. 7–30 and therefore during the lifetime of Jesus, there is told the story of one Taxo and his sons who, during persecution of the servants of God, deliberately give themselves over to a martyr death, "and *then* his kingdom shall appear throughout all creation" (Ch. 10).

Hence it is not true to say that Jewish tradition repelled the idea of suffering prior to the establishment of the kingdom. What can be said is this: that it did not conceive of a suffering Messiah or a Messianic people, and with all the more reason it did not admit the possibility of suffering in the kingdom of God.

Jesus, however, shattered this view. In the key passage of Mark 8:27–35, the confession of Peter at Caesarea Philippi, after accepting the title "Messiah," Jesus proceeds immediately to teach his disciples that, "the Son of Man was destined to suffer grievously. . . ."

If we recall the glorious image that the "Son of Man" motif evoked from Daniel, and its relation to the "kingdom" delivered at the end of time to the saints (Dan 7:13, 18), we can grasp some of the shattering contradiction-in-terms that this saying of Jesus implied for the disciples, and why Peter understandably took Jesus aside and chided him on being out of his mind. Jesus' response is that Peter here is the instrument of Satan. In the context of the kingdom, this means that the idea of a Messiah or a kingdom without suffering is really a hoax propagandized by the great eschatological adversary of the kingdom — Satan!

Mark immediately adds that Jesus says not only that he must suffer, but that his disciples must be willing to suffer as well (Mk 8:34). Here, then, is another instance of Jesus' jolting his hearers from a false mythology into the realism of everyday life and the necessity of facing the really critical issue: are you willing to suffer and die with me?

And here too we may speak of the passages in Matthew 10:34–36 and Luke 12:49–53 in which Jesus, having come to cast fire upon the earth, brings a sword instead of peace, division instead of unity. He does not bring a miraculous delivery from the mutual alienations among men which we saw erupting and degenerating in Genesis. As the eschatological crisis came to a head in his own death upon the cross, so will it also be for his followers. He has come indeed to heal, but he shatters once again the thought that mankind can be healed in any other way than by the cruel realism of a head-on confrontation with suffering and death.

The same thrust is given in the novel way in which the miracles of Jesus are treated in Matthew 8:16–17. That evening they brought him many who were possessed by devils. He cast out the spirits with a word and cured all who were sick. This was to fulfill the prophecy of Isaiah: *He took our sicknesses away and carried our diseases for us.* Matthew wishes to show that in the miracles of Jesus, his character of Servant of Yahweh was shown most clearly. They are works less of divine power than of human compassion and mercy — or better, the divine power is most shown forth in the compassionate nature of these works of Jesus. The Greek *ebastasen* can mean either "bore the burden of" or "took away." While there is no evidence that Jesus himself suffered any of the diseases he cured, he did take these ills upon himself by compassionately identifying himself with them (as Matthew often insists), and it was *thus* that he took them away.

Finally, another important datum of the New Testament must be faced: Jesus' withdrawal from his disciples and this world through the ascension. This dimension of the New Testament may cause us difficulty both in our understanding of the Christian mystery and in our attempts to teach it and preach it. For if there is anything that is branded today as cowardice by a world caught up in the anguishing problems of man, it is withdrawal, disinvolvement. And at first sight it looks as if this is just what the ascension is: a withdrawal from this world to the next.

Yet we do know that Jesus got involved with the human situation to its utmost — unto death on a cross. Why then did he withdraw his presence if he had the power to make it permanent? A parent who does everything for his child when that child should be doing most things for himself does not really love the child. The educator who does not challenge the student to do ultimately for himself what the teacher has been doing for him fails as an educator. The function of a parent and of an educator is ultimately to make himself dispensable.

So with Christ. The disciples had been so mesmerized by his magnetic personality, so awe-struck by his miraculous powers, that even after his resurrection — even at the moment of his ascension, according to Luke in Acts — they asked him if he were on the point of setting up this miraculous kingdom of God. The answer was that they themselves would be endued with *power* through the coming of the Holy Spirit, and they would continue the work of Christ, they would be his presence in the world. It was necessary for him to be absent in order to be present in a new way. The Holy Spirit is the presence of the risen and exalted Christ to his disciples and to the world. Christianity, they had to learn, is not just Jesus of Nazareth but the visible *community* gathered in his name. And Christianity does not mean letting Jesus solve their problems by working magical feats for them while they sit by and watch, but rather means being possessed by his own power within them to do the works he did. And the meaning is the same today. The Ascension is our weaning; Pentecost, our coming of age.

IV. The Apostolic Kerygma and the Kingdom of God

In the preaching of the apostolic Church (which we also have reflected in the Synoptics) we find a rarer use of the concept "kingdom of God." But when it is used, it contains both present and futuristic elements — the apostolic Church now pointing to the death-resurrection of Jesus and His sending of the Spirit as affirmation of the *present* reality of the kingdom, the Parousia or Second Coming as affirmation of the *future* consummation.

But there is something in the method of the apostolic preaching more significant for our inquiry — although it may not be immediately evident how this affects the theology of the secular. It is this: the Apostolic Church not only preached the words of Jesus and his deeds. She freely reinterpreted them. Any serious book on the parables will show how the

Church adapted, edited, contracted and expanded the parables of Jesus with sovereign freedom. An explanation is added, words are recast, and even the same parable is reused and a different point is drawn from it. Moreover, it is very hard to say just where in the Gospels, if anywhere, we have the words of Jesus just as they fell from his mouth. At times a whole motif will be transferred into a different key more suitable to an audience — as for example John will use "eternal life" where the synoptics used "kingdom of God." And the deeds of Jesus will be re-interpreted and the narration modified to suit the needs of the audience to which they are addressed.

What does all this mean? Simply that the Apostles in their preaching did just what Jesus did in his: they seized upon motifs and concepts relevant to their listeners and then, convinced that the Holy Spirit within them was sufficient link with the message of Jesus, they spoke a relevant message. Certainly they preached Jesus, they preached about his passion and death and resurrection, about the need for conversion and baptism and all the rest. But there was a sovereign freedom in the *formulation* of that message. Continuity with Jesus was essential, but mere continuity of terms could be a betrayal of that very message *if* the cultural context was so different that the old words, even had they been said by Jesus, were meaningless or misleading.

We shall return to this problem in the final chapter. But it needs to be said here because doubtless the reader is wondering when a conclusion is going to be drawn about the synoptics' theology of the secular. From what we have seen, we can say that if we look to the Gospels, and specifically to the central theme of the kingdom of God, for a clue to resolve the tension between a this-worldly and an other-worldly concern, we will not find it. The dynamo of the New Testament kerygma, whether in the preaching of Jesus or the Apostles, depends for its energy on the tension of these two poles. To an audience which defines life in terms of amassing riches and pleasures here and now Jesus says, "Wake up — God's kingdom is at hand." To those whom the expectation of the kingdom lulled into a complacent passivity Jesus says, "Wake up — the kingdom is here — can't you see it beginning?"

What is significant, it seems to me, at any stage of the Bible, is to ask what was the cultural motif that the prophet or the sacred writer seized upon, and then to discover what he did with it. We have seen at every step that the Old Testament, and now the Synoptics themselves, are constantly using current concepts but "demythologizing" them toward a more realistic view of man. My contention is that the "timeless" message of Scripture, if we can even speak of such, is to be found more in this *thrust,* in this *emergence* than in the content considered statically.

The relevance of this for our modern problem of the secular world will, I hope, become clear when I offer a theological theory which will attempt to do greater justice to the actual facts of the formation of the Bible than some of the theories advanced in the past.

4. Paul: Christ and the Cosmos

I. The Otherworldliness of Paul

At first sight Paul seems to have little concern with this-worldly pursuits. Particularly in his first letters, he seems to be so preoccupied with the coming Parousia that little room is left for speculation about the interim. We may have particular difficulty comprehending the ancient type of space travel which Paul seems to reflect in 1 Thessalonians 4:16–17: "At the trumpet of God, the voice of the archangel will call out the command and the Lord himself will come down from heaven; those who have died in Christ will be the first to rise, and then those of us who are still alive will be taken up in the clouds, together with them, to meet the Lord in the air."

Now there are some who would say that Paul urges a retreat from the world, that he presents the Church as the haven in which we are to find refuge until the storm of life is past, and that really all we need do is to await the appearance of this cosmic spaceship and our own individualized Dick Tracy type of flying wastebasket to take off and meet it. This is obviously a caricature, but it no doubt represents some of the fantastic gymnastics of imagination which many of the people in the pews go through when we read this epistle at Requiem Masses.

Let me first say that this particular passage illustrates the problem we have been encountering in each of the preceding chapters: that of the cultural context and that of the formal thrust. Paul is here using the traditional imagery of apocalyptic and is speaking according to the mentality, especially the Jewish mentality, of the Thessalonian community. The ancients did not think in abstractions. Where we would say "the eschatological call to judgment," Paul says "trumpet of God," echoing an Exodus motif (Ex 19:13, 16, 19) and "voice of archangel," illustrating the grandiose nature of this assembly call, just as the sergeant who sounds the bugle to assemble the troops is not the general who reviews them. Where we would say "it will be the final encounter where we will face Christ the Lord," Paul says, "the Lord will come down from heaven." Where we would say, "the just will share in his divine glory," Paul says, "we will ride the clouds with those who have preceded us in death and will join the Son of Man who comes on the clouds of heaven." The concrete image expresses graphically what we are accustomed to think of in more abstract terms, and I'm not sure that our abstraction is an improvement, for our faith tells us that the ultimate reality is not an abstraction at all but a very real, personal and concrete *experience*. But it is important that we not transfer woodenly the cultural context of Paul's time to ours without the theological meaning. The latter remains the same even though today we would conceive and express it in different terms.

But even supposing we solve this problem via semantics, what about the theology itself? Does Paul's eschatology urge a retreat from the world? There are some passages which surely seem to point in that direction: "When the Lord does punish us, it is to correct us and stop us from being *condemned with the world*" (1 Cor 11:32). "Has not God made foolish the wisdom of this world?" (1 Cor 1:20.) And then, of course, there is the passage always cited in this discussion, that recommending celibacy or virginity because of the imminence of the Parousia (1 Cor 7:25–35). With Christ so near, what's the use of getting involved with this-worldly concerns?

If this is true, if Paul's eschatology does urge a retreat from the world, then he could be accused of having nothing to say to the modern generation — to today's college students, for example, who are more moved by Watts and Selma than they are by the thought of an apocalyptic Armageddon. My own experience in teaching the epistles of Paul to college students today has impressed me quite to the contrary — that Paul is very relevant and meaningful to today's young Christian adults, once they are given enough background to cut through the semantic obstacles that face the unprepared man-in-the-pew. Once again, the proper understanding of Paul comes not from the cultural motifs he used but in what he did with them.

Even in Thessalonians, Paul corrects an infantile interpretation of the imminent Parousia by insisting that the certainty of the coming judgment, far from justifying a passive complacency, rather fires the Christian to "make the most of his time."[1] The thought of the Parousia impels Paul to think of the supreme importance of living by a dynamic *love* — a love that not only does all it has to, but overflows its level and pours itself out in working both for one's fellow Christians and for *all* men. This intent appears clearly from the prayer in 1 Thessalonians:

> May God our Father himself, and our Lord Jesus Christ, make it easy for us to come to you. May the Lord be generous in increasing your love and make you love one another and the whole human race as much as we love you. And may he so confirm your hearts in holiness that you may be blameless in the sight of our God and Father when our Lord Jesus Christ comes with all his saints (1 Thes 3:11–13).

Thus Paul's eschatology leads to and emphasizes the crucial importance of the *present* in the Christian life under the sign of the Parousia, and he describes the central activity of this present as that of love — fraternal and universal love, which is a gift of the Father and of the Lord who is returning. Thus, at this point, we can already conclude that Paul's eschatology does not discourage all types of this-worldly

---

[1] Movies like *High Noon* and *Ikiru* have exploited the theme of impending crisis to show how this can intensify man's use of the interim.

involvement. There is an involvement which is essential and urgent: the involvement of love.

Only from this point of view does Paul's recommendation of celibacy make any sense:

> About remaining celibate, I have no directions from the Lord but give my own opinion as one who, by the Lord's mercy, has stayed faithful. Well then, I believe that in these present times of stress this is right: that it is good for a man to stay as he is. If you are tied to a wife, do not look for freedom; if you are free of a wife, then do not look for one. But if you marry, it is no sin, and it is not a sin for a young girl to get married. They will have their troubles, though, in their married life, and I should like to spare you that.

> Brothers, that is what I mean: our time is growing short. Those who have wives should live as though they had none, and those who mourn should live as though they had nothing to mourn for; those who are enjoying life should live as though there were nothing to laugh about; those whose life is buying things should live as though they had nothing of their own; and those who have to deal with the world should not become engrossed in it. I say this because the world as we know it is passing away.

> I would like to see you free from all worry. An unmarried man can devote himself to the Lord's affairs, all he need worry about is pleasing the Lord. But a married man has to bother about the world's affairs and devote himself to pleasing his wife; he is torn two ways. In the same way an unmarried woman, like a young girl, can devote herself to the Lord's affairs; all she need worry about is being holy in body and spirit. The married woman, on the other hand, has to worry about the world's affairs and devote herself to pleasing her husband. I say this only to help you, not to put a halter round your necks, but simply to make sure that everything is as it should be, and that you give your undivided attention to the Lord (1 Cor 7:24–35).

To interpret this message as a distrust of things sexual is to miss the point. The advantage of virginity derives uniquely from Christian eschatology and not from a pessimistic theology of the flesh. And the question is not whether a Christian is going to get involved or not. It is merely a question of what kind of involvement he is going to choose. Every Christian's existence presents a twofold dimension: incarnational and eschatological — or, to avoid those technical terms, a dimension by which he belongs to this world, and a dimension by which he belongs to the next. The married person is necessarily and by duty involved with the things of this world in the sense that he is committed to his spouse. He too, however, must look to the consummation of his Christian existence not only *through* the present involvement but also *beyond* it. And thus he will as a Christian continue to be a pilgrim. He will hold his goods with a relaxed grasp, valuing them indeed, but ready to release them when his Lord calls. In other words, even in his involvement there must be freedom.

The virgin or celibate is likewise involved, Paul says. But the involvement is a more direct one in the "concerns of the Lord," namely his kingdom and its coming on earth. By the "worldly interests" of which the celibate is free Paul makes clear he is thinking of concern for one's spouse. This is not the only nor even the chief meaning of "secular" today, for the latter term evokes a much broader scope of community, national, and international welfare. Inasmuch as these are the Lord's interest (and they certainly are), there is no reason why the celibate cannot and should not be creatively involved with them. Just as there must be freedom in the involvement of the married, so there must be involvement in the freedom of the celibate.

Of course, we would have missed the point if we should take Paul's distinction to imply that concern for one's spouse is in no way the Lord's interest, for we know from Ephesians 5 that for the married such a concern is his interest. We are brought back again to the fact that the Christian life as such, prior to the "states" in which it finds expression, is both incarnational and eschatological: It has a dimension of involvement and one of freedom. What the married and the celibate states specify is the particular *sign* or *witness* that each gives to one of these dimensions, the married to the dimension of involvement, the celibate to the dimension of freedom.

The married couple witness in a special way to the value of the things of this world because they make the direct concern for these part of their pledge to one another. In this way, by identifying themselves with the temporal order, they testify to the repeated refrain of Genesis: "God saw that they were good." Their mutual union, consecrated by the grace of Christ, stands as a witness and a safeguard of the divinely established value of this state, against all forms of angelism. They likewise show by their lives that the achievement of unity and unicity in marriage (so longed for by the author of Genesis and demanded by our Lord) is indeed possible, with its attendant joys and happiness. Moreover, married love is a sign of Christ's union with his Church, and hence must be a visible union (Eph 5). Marriage, then, is essential to the Church's life in this world, which is a world of signs. And because it is a sign of the union of Christ and his Church, it is also a sign of the consecrated celibate's own union with Christ; and since it is the nature of a sign to *signify*, that is, to communicate knowledge, the celibate will learn from Christian marriage how to love God. If proof of this relation is needed, one has only to observe the fact that most solid religious vocations come from homes where the ideal of Christian marriage has been to some extent achieved. Psychologically speaking, one might say that only when one experiences the fulfillment which Christ brings to a truly Christian home can one begin to suspect and to desire the transcendent Reality which lies beyond the experienced reality, that ultimate Reality to which the visible reality points.

The state of consecrated celibacy in its turn has its own sign value. It witnesses to the fact that there is a fulfillment yet to come, a fulfillment so real that it can be anticipated, by way of a sign, here and now. And thus consecrated celibacy becomes a unique witness to the Reality of God in the world. As someone has put it, marriage makes some sense (not a great deal, but *some sense*) if God doesn't exist. But religious life doesn't make a bit of sense. And herein lies its unique value as a sign.

But what of the temporal or secular value of celibacy? If the married state is a sign and guardian of the inherent value of this world and a witness that sinking one's roots into it is worthwhile, the consecrated celibate is a sign of *freedom within the world*. More than that, the virginal state stands as a constant stimulus even to the married state to grow constantly and to progress: a reminder that no achievement of love in this world can ever be labeled "enough," but has within it a greater achievement yet, even here in this world, as it is drawn toward the source and consummation of all love, God, who is Love itself. Recently when one of my fellow religious in a moment of despondency confided to a married woman that he thought religious life was on the way out, she pinned him against the wall and lectured him for ten minutes on what his witness as a religious meant to her as a Christian wife and a mother. He confided to me that this impassioned lecture made him realize as never before his witness to the Church. Thus the witness of marriage and consecrated celibacy admirably complement one another: the one which stresses the genuine goodness of this world, the other which stresses the *freedom* and *creativity* that the Christian has to deploy within it.

Such is the dense thought underlying Paul's theology of marriage and virginity. In the light of the so-called identity-crisis of celibacy in our times (which is merely the result of an eternally prolonged but rapidly dissolving identity crisis of Christian marriage), it is important to stress not only that Christian marriage but also that Christian celibacy and virginity have a crucial contribution to make even to the theology of the secular.

There is another way in which Paul uses the eschatological motif. We recall how the synoptics use the Parousia motif to urge watchfulness. Paul does the same (1 Thes 5:1–11).

However, he goes beyond the synoptics in one significant way. The synoptics had compared the suddenness of Christ's coming to that of the thief who breaks in at night (Mt 24:43) and Paul does too (1 Thes 5:3). But then he goes on to add:

> But it is not as if you live in the dark, my brothers, for that Day to overtake you like a thief. No, you are all sons of light and sons of the day: we do not belong to the night or to darkness, so we should not go on sleeping, as everyone else does, but stay wide awake and sober (1 Thes 5:4-6).

Paul wishes to correct the excessive impression of fear or complete extrinsicism which Christians might read into the "sudden as a thief" image. Christians should be alert not because they might be surprised or "caught" by Christ's sudden return, but rather because the Parousia corresponds to what they are essentially as Christians. As the fish seeks water or a trapped miner light and air, so the Christian aspires for the Parousia. Christ's coming is not an ambush but a consummation. We are on the road which will issue in Paul's "existential" moral theology — namely, that the moral imperative for the Christian is to act not because of some extrinsic law or obligation, but rather simply because of what he *is*. "Become what you are!"

II. THE WORLDLINESS OF PAUL

For all that we must admit that Paul's early letters are predominated by the thought of the Parousia, of the glorious Christ whose resurrection announces his Second Coming. In the major epistles — Corinthians, Galatians and Romans — there is a perceptible shift toward the present, the Christian life as lived here and now. Several themes appear now and are developed at length: particularly a theology of the cross and the sacramental life as a death and resurrection with Christ.

How Paul's own apostolic experiences contributed to this inward deepening of his theology is amply treated elsewhere,[2]

---

[2] Cf., for example, Lucien Cerfaux, *Christ in the Theology of St. Paul* (New York: Herder and Herder, 1958), pp. 107-160.

and we can spare repeating it here. The theology of the Cross and of co-suffering with Christ is a much more realistic view of the Christian and apostolic life as it was actually experienced in the early communities. It was simply the extension to the Church of Jesus' own demythologizing of the kingdom, namely that life in Christ, possessing all the Messianic goods promised of old, particularly the abundant outpouring of the Holy Spirit, is not presently an escape from suffering nor even from witnessing unto death; as Paul and Barnabas tell the new communities at Lystra, Iconium, and Antioch of Pisidia: "We all have to experience many hardships before we enter the kingdom of God" (Acts 14:22). But the glory of suffering is not merely that it is a necessary pre-condition for the kingdom; the Christian *co-suffers* with Christ, "sharing his sufferings so as to share his glory" (Rom 8:17).

But the development which is most significant for the modern question about the theology of the secular is, I believe, the emergence of the *Body of Christ* theme.[3] The term *body* of Christ refers first, of course, to Christ's own physical body now glorious. To this one body Christians are joined organically through Baptism (1 Cor 12:13) and are nourished unto its unity through the Eucharist (1 Cor 10:17). Thus the Church becomes the Body of Christ, one organic person with him.

In the Greek philosophic system, bodiliness is what accounts for separateness and individuality; it limits form or perfection. In the Jewish mind of Paul, however, the opposite is true. *Body* means solidarity. It evokes our solidarity with the created universe and also our solidarity with our fellow Christians and with our fellowman. The cosmic or earthly solidarity appears from the first pages of the Bible, when we are told that Adam is formed from the dust of the earth. Rabbinic tradition developed this line of thinking by affirming

---

[3] See my *Living Thought of St. Paul* (Milwaukee: The Bruce Publishing Co., 1966), pp. 174–177.

that the dust God used to form Adam's body was taken not just from one spot but from all over the earth, thus illustrating all mankind's radical solidarity and the fact that there was really no natural difference between a man from the east or from the west. Thus a social solidarity grew from the cosmic one, and the term *body* was apt to describe it. Thus in Heb 13:3 we read, "Keep in mind those who are in prison, as though you were in prison with them, and those who are being badly treated, since you too are in the one *body*."

But Paul is also aware of the cosmic dimension of the term *body,* and it appears as early as Romans in that significant passage in 8:18–25:

> I think that what we suffer in this life can never be compared to the glory, as yet unrevealed, which is waiting for us. The whole creation is eagerly waiting for God to reveal his sons. It was not for any fault on the part of creation that it was made unable to attain its purpose — the subjection came from him who enslaved it — but creation still retains the hope of being freed, like us, from its slavery to decadence, to enjoy the same freedom and glory as the children of God. From the beginning till now the entire creation, as we know, has been groaning and travailing in one great act of giving birth; and not only creation, but all of us who possess the first-fruits of the Spirit, we too groan inwardly as we wait for our *body* to be set free.[4]

Here there is an obvious intent to stress the solidarity of creation with man both in the fall and in the redemption. The passage occurs in a context of explaining why present suffering is part of the lot of Christians: the Christian and the world are both locked in the same agony: the agony which is "one great act of giving birth," which, of course, is the issuing in of the cosmic redemption: and the whole process is called the redemption of the *body*.

The term body, then, in Paul, means the Christian solidarity with everything human and with all creation. In Romans, creation is pictured, as it were, in the bleachers cheering the

---

[4] Here I have made some minor modifications in the Jerusalem Bible translation.

Christian on in his eschatological struggle with Satan and the forces of evil which have divorced man and through man creation itself from its fulfillment in God. Creation thus is on man's side — and any fear the Christian might have of creation as such (and man's better knowledge and use of it) is not only ungrounded, it is very false. You do not win a ball game by killing your cheerleaders.

Paul had to "demythologize" creation for many of his converts, particularly in the area of foods, clean and unclean (for the Jews) and sacralized or not for the converted gentiles (the idol offerings). It was just this specific situation that led him to that declaration of Christian (and human) freedom: "For me there are no forbidden things" (1 Cor 6:12). All creation is *for* the Christian, just as God is (Rom 8:31). The alienation has been healed on all levels: "Paul, Apollos, Cephas, the world, life and death, the present and the future, all are your servants; but you belong to Christ and Christ belongs to God" (1 Cor 3:22–23). Baptism not only makes the Christian belong to God; it makes the universe belong to the Christian.

If then God has been presented at times as a God who fears that his own universe will lead man away from him, and fears man's knowledge of it, then it is better if this God is dead, for he is not the true God of revelation nor the God of our universe.

All of this is beautifully deepened in the later captivity epistles.[5] Here the Church is defined as "the fullness (*pleroma*) of him who is achieving his cosmic proportions through all his members" (Eph 1:23; my translation). To understand what Paul means by *pleroma,* it is necessary to think in terms of a dynamic fullness. The Stoics spoke of the world being a fullness, they even called it the fullness of God, or vice versa, God is the fullness of the universe. But for them this was pantheism, that is, the static identification of nature

---

[5] Cf. my *Maturing in Christ* (Milwaukee: Bruce IMPACT Books, 1964), final chapter.

with God, the world itself being the only reality, and self-contained. It operated according to fixed and immutable laws, and man's perfection consisted in submitting to these inevitable laws and dominating his passions in order to do so. Man in a sense became superior to change by accepting it and striving to rise above it. What this really meant, however, is that in submitting to this god which was nature, man was submitting to the old cyclic return, and abandoning hope of breaking out to a really new existence.

While Paul was surely aware of this meaning of *pleroma* (many of the notions of the philosophers were popularized in his day), he certainly did not make use of it, except to dethrone or "demythologize" it. His meaning of *fullness* goes back to the Old Testament notion: God fills heaven and earth with his creative fullness, that is, he has poured his power and glory into every bit of the universe. Not identified with it, he is rather the maker of it, ever sustaining it by his continuing creative presence. This is what we mean by saying that the notion of pleroma or fullness in Paul is a dynamic concept.

Now God has made all his fullness to dwell bodily in Christ (Col 2:10). This means that the fullness of his creative and historic power has been centered in Christ — bodily: not merely in his person individually, but in such a way that it flows over into his members: "In his body lives the fullness of divinity, and in him you too find your own fulfillment" (Col 2:9). The Church, in turn, is Christ's fullness, that is, she receives continually from Christ the divine life flowing into him from the Father (as in Jn 1:16: full of grace and truth, and of his fullness we have all received).

But now comes the important point for our inquiry: the *pleroma* is a dynamic concept, and it is basically, I think, because of the cosmic dimension that Paul introduces into it. At the end of the succession of basins receiving and passing on the waters of divine life stands the world itself, ultimate beneficiary of the action. The Church, the Body of Christ, is the immediate minister of this presence to the world. This is the meaning of that passage which defines the Church as "the fullness of him who is achieving his cosmic proportions through all his members" (Eph 1:23, my translation). Christ, Servant of Yahweh, has come to minister salvation not merely to the people of God but through them to the world. It is terribly easy for us, the new people of God, to fall into the exclusivism for which Jesus excoriated his contemporaries, and to think that salvation stops with us, the visible Church. No, Paul says, "God in Christ was reconciling the *world* to himself" (2 Cor 5:19). And therefore the Christian is one who is governed by two poles: Christ from whom and in whom he exists, and the world to which he is sent and for which he also exists: to redeem it, as Jesus did, by *serving*.

At times, of course, the progressive redemption of the universe is described in terms of a struggle with the cosmic powers, thus as a conquest. It is practically the old synoptic theme of exorcism expanded to a cosmic scale. Behind the figure, however, is the reality that this struggle is one of Christ in his members to make effective Christ's lordship over his people and thus to achieve their freedom. It is thus a conquest in the sense of freeing man from the elements which enslave him in this world.

Paul's concept of *pleroma* may be illustrated thus:

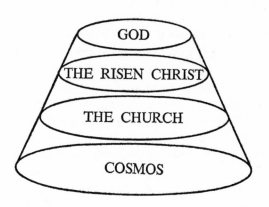

This must not be viewed statically but dynamically — as a process continually going on. God established this plan in time through the incarnation, death and resurrection of his Son and the establishment of the Church. These are past events as far as their constitution is concerned, but they are living and operative realities right now — God is pouring his life into Christ, Christ into the Church, the Church into the world. When the process is complete, God will be "all in all" (1 Cor 15:28). The pleroma is the dynamic or functional dimension of what Paul describes elsewhere in these terms: "The universe is yours, and you are Christ's and Christ is God's" (1 Cor 3:22 f.).

But what is meant by the universe in Paul? Surely by it he means the totality of beings, no matter whether material or spiritual. And thus there is a true cosmic mystique in Paul. Yet there can be no doubt that for Paul the crucial center of this world is man, and thus even the cosmic sweep is eminently soteriological — the universe is saved when man is saved; the universe finds its meaning when man finds the Christological center of his authentic existence. To put it bluntly, I don't think Paul would care very much whether we got to the moon or not — *unless* this venture served mankind. It is important to stress this lest we fall into a false cosmic mysticism at the expense of mankind itself — and build pyramids at the price of enslaving mankind.

This conclusion is supported by the fact that for Paul the essential cosmifying and unifying activity is *love*. "Love builds" (1 Cor 8:1). What a program is contained in those two words! The new world to be built will not be the automatic process of an inevitable evolution. Nor can it be had by turning on a switch — although the destruction of the cosmos may be had that way. It can be built only by a conscious unifying of wills in the pursuit of the common goal — with all the corporate asceticism that calls for. Thus, after showing that the aim of Christ's ascension to the Father was that he might become the source of the world's "fullness,"

Paul goes on to show how it is achieved: "If we live by the truth and in love, we shall grow in all ways into Christ, who is the head by whom the whole body is fitted and joined together, every joint adding its own strength, for each separate part to work according to its function. So the body grows until it has built itself up, in love" (Eph 4:15–16).

CONCLUSION

If Paul's thought is in any way normative for the contemporary Church, it schools us to avoid two extremes when we approach the Christian theology of the secular: the extreme of identifying Christian concern only with the next world, and the other extreme of identifying it totally with this world.

The temptation has been very great in the past history of the Church to identify the Church and the pursuit of Christian perfection and for that matter God himself with the next life, heaven, the un-worldly world. And no doubt there are Christians today who continue to make a schizophrenic division between their necessarily worldly activity and their faith. On the other hand, the thrust toward the temporal, toward the worldly, the secular, may likewise have its pitfalls if it identifies God with the world. God has indeed identified himself with the world in the incarnation and death of Christ — but not in a pantheistic way. His entry into history has always been and remains a sovereignly free act in its origin, and he stands outside the world not as a disinterested spectator but rather as a Father urging an infant to walk and holding his arms out to receive him. God is the goal to which the world must move, and therefore is the ultimate guarantor and stimulus of its growth and evolution. This is a crucial point; it is the only description that does justice to the biblical God, who is the God of the future.
Bible does not use these theological terms, it is true. Rather
God thus remains transcendent in his immanence. The

we are presented on the one hand, with the utter freedom and gratuity of God's intervention (which reveals his transcendence), and on the other hand, the fact of total involvement and identification with all that is human in the Body of Christ (his historical immanence). Now these two poles of the divine activity are reflected in that dynamism which God has given to the Church: charity, love. Poured into the Church by God (Rom 5:5), it has the paradoxical traits of God's own sovereign freedom and total involvement.

Its willingness to identify itself with everything human, to be compassionate, to suffer with, appears abundantly in the Pauline epistles, but particularly in the hymn to eternal charity in 1 Corinthians 13. It was this love which led Christ to his death: "He loved me and gave himself up for me" (Gal 2:20).

But the beauty of this immense act of loving sacrifice is that it was sovereignly free. And so is charity. Because the Christian stimulus to identification with the world comes from without, in virtue of a higher power, it does not lose itself in the world but remains creatively active there. We can call this the eschatological dimension of charity, namely that which points to an end beyond the immediate achievement. It finds, as we have seen, a particular expression in the state of consecrated virginity, a special sign of the eschatological freedom of charity. What is important to realize is that this freedom, this transcendence, this eschatological dimension, is the condition for charity's real contribution to the world. For precisely because of this divine origin and end, charity cannot be defeated by the collapse of any of its human projects. It has an uncanny power to survive human defeat, to rise from the ashes, to start over. Paul himself realized this when, in Romans, he wrote:

> After saying this, what can we add? With God on our side who can be against us? Since God did not spare his own Son, but gave him up to benefit us all, we may be certain, after such a gift, that he will not refuse anything he can give. Could anyone accuse those that God has chosen? When God acquits, could

anyone condemn? Could Christ Jesus? No! He not only died for us — he rose from the dead, and there at God's right hand he stands and pleads for us.

Nothing therefore can come between us and the love of Christ, even if we are troubled or worried, or being persecuted, or lacking food or clothes, or being threatened or even attacked. As scripture promises: *For your sake we are being massacred daily, and reckoned as sheep for the slaughter.* These are the trials through which we triumph, by the power of him who loved us.

For I am certain of this: neither death nor life, no angel, no prince, nothing that exists, nothing still to come, not any power, or height or depth, nor any created thing, can ever come between us and the love of God made visible in Christ Jesus our Lord (Rom 8:31–39).

5. What Does It Mean Today?

Today's world weighs everything in the scales of relevance. And the Bible has not escaped the weighing. In this final chapter I should like to draw together some of the major directions we have uncovered and to suggest what all of it may mean for our contemporary situation. Each reader would doubtless do it differently, and there is certainly nothing final or sacred about what follows.

I. THE GOD OF THE FUTURE

The first conception of God that emerged from the early documents was that underlying the name Yahweh. It was, on the one hand, a refusal to conceptualize God and, on the other, an affirmation that he would reveal himself in the events to come. Here was the seed already of the future hope; it also, however, left the future open-ended — not merely the perpetual return of the natural seasons, but a free and undetermined possibility to create a historical future without limitations. Israel would never abide the idea that man's existence consists in resigning himself to the inevitable laws of nature or to the folly of fate. Yahweh is a God of liberation, who can break the fetters of man, whatever they be. This schooled Israel to a sense of superiority to nature and even to historical odds of great magnitude. While the ultimate victory lies in the hands of Yahweh, to whom will go all the glory of victory, nevertheless, in Israel mankind began to breathe a new air of freedom because the fetishes and fears of mysterious divine powers in nature or in the stars were being progressively dispersed by a ruthless monotheism that pitilessly hacked down the pretended sacredness of anything that was not God.

This is why the biblical God is not one who saps human nature of its energies through the promotion of an "escapist" faith, but rather one who challenges and empowers man to be truly man. Israel came to look upon idolatry and magic as dehumanizing and enslaving and upon its God as the God of freedom, the God who enables man to be man, to regain his mastery of himself and of the world. God is thus aligned with genuine humanity. To find him is to find life.

But Yahwistic faith was not merely iconoclastic and liberating. It also opened man's view to a real, progressive, or, to use current terminology, *evolutionary* view of man and his history. And perhaps today this is precisely the view of God we need to recapture: God as God of the future. We have become so accustomed to thinking of God as doing all his saving activity, like his creative activity, in the past — or at most his "renewing" it for us sacramentally in the present — that we may not have adequately emphasized the future dimension of our faith. By this I mean not only the final consummation of the next life, but the very real steps which God is urging us to take today to bring about the better world of tomorrow. Far from wondering whether God's interests might be compromised by an evolving universe, we ought perhaps to take more seriously his invitation and prodding to *make* it evolve through free and creative action now. In other words, if we take "I Am who I Am" seriously, God does not follow and try to catch up with evolution; he leads it and produces it. Who more than his own people should be prepared to pick up the cadence and lead the evolutionary process?

But there are two qualifications that should be made in this connection. The first is that the evolution of the world has reached a point where the next step is not going to be an automatic thing. The "leaps" of which Teilhard de Chardin speaks in his grandiose drama of evolution may justify extrapolating optimistically into the future. But since the appearance of man on earth, a new element has entered: the noosphere or rational action. Where the human race goes from here will depend largely on where it decides to go. And we must not exclude the real possibility of self-alienation. Granted that there are powerful centripetal forces impelling to world unity, there are also powerful centrifugal forces. The unity of mankind, with all that involves of sharing and peace, cannot be achieved without the lucid and free and constructive activity of man.

It is precisely here that the Judaeo-Christian view of man as a free agent under God has such an important contribution to make. For the new world to happen, it has to be willed. Any other view ultimately falls back into pagan determinism or fate. But the vastness and complexity of the operation, the seeming hopelessness of it, may lead us to adopt the attitude of passivity which *seems* to be the more religious view. It was that of Jesus' contemporaries: God will solve the problem in his own good time; if the kingdom is to come, it will come without our doing anything about it. But we saw that Jesus himself struggled to dethrone that idol. The kingdom of God, he said, is within your grasp.

Now Jesus reduced all valid human activity to love. And love, Paul hastens to add, *builds*. The love which the Christian professes and strives to live more fully is not a mere gentle disposition toward all. It is essentially an activity which seeks the good of the community to which it belongs and engages man's intelligence in planning and achieving that good. For this is what is meant by *building*.

Love, it is true, is a word so used of late that it has worn thin to near meaninglessness. It often means "whatever is convenient for me at the moment," and this amounts to a curious situation in which it is ironically true that "Love covers a multitude of sins." Others take love to mean the humanitarian concern of the beatnik who worries about the world's hungry and homeless and war-victims but is unwilling to get involved in any human structure to really do something about it. But this is not Christian love. Christian love *builds*. It addresses itself with intelligence and involvement to strengthen weak structures, to exorcise and purify those that need it, to build new ones where there are none.

We are at a stage of history eminently ripe for the message of the love that builds. There was a time — and we are not out of it yet — when it was thought both inside and outside the Church that structure could replace love. Happily, we have, I think, passed this stage, or we are passing it. We know pretty well what we don't want — our literature is full of it, almost *ad nauseam*. But we are not yet sure we know what we want by way of a better replacement. This explains much of the unrest in the Church today. Nevertheless, I am beginning to think we are outgrowing the reaction stage of "love without structure." We are on the verge of discovering, I hope, that *love builds*.

This leads to the second observation concerning the evolutionary process. Love, like Christ, does not come to destroy but to fulfill. That is to say, it comes not, as it were, to speak a foreign tongue to man but rather first to take on totally the human situation it wishes to help. There is no redemption without incarnation. Love, like God, not only listens but shares the lot of those to whom it comes.

This means that wherever good is lacking, wherever there is misery and suffering, love comes first of all to share that suffering, and in sharing to heal. But more than that, it also means that whatever there is of good in the world is embraced by Christian love.

II. THE REDEMPTION OF OUR BODY

Such is the incarnational nature of love. It does not seek to save souls but to save men. The "Body" theology of St. Paul elaborates this in function of the life of the Church in the world. The redemption of man is a redemption of his body (Rom 8:23); the body is joined to Christ (1 Cor 6:17), the Christian is joined by baptism to the risen body of Christ (1 Cor 12:13), and the transforming Spirit that he progressively receives through that body-union transforms his entire being (2 Cor 3:18). This means a healing of man in all his dimensions: the alienations he experiences are progressively healed and man finds himself when he finds God in Christ. By the same token, anything that helps man to recover himself is all part of the "body-activity" which Christian love seeks and supports. This is simply the Pauline way of affirming the message of the Gospels — that the signs of the coming of God's kingdom in the person of Jesus are the healings of men's bodies and minds, the first step in the binding of Satan.

No truly humanizing activity can then be indifferent, no matter what its source. It does not even need to bear the label "Christian."

But body theology also means solidarity with one's fellowman and with the society of which he is part. This would apply first, of course, to the Christian community which is the Church. But it does not stop there. It embraces all mankind — not merely because of some external law that we must love all men, but simply because we are locked in inescapable solidarity with every man on the face of the earth, and charity simply confirms and intensifies this belonging.

"Body" too embraces the physical cosmos. It is an extension of man, so to speak. There is a genuine mystique in Christianity for putting the imprint of redemption on the physical world. Man's sense of inadequacy before the physical powers of the universe does not correspond to God's ideal plan for him. And thus man's effort to gain control of the universe and to make it serve him, far from being essentially a danger to his recovery of selfhood, is really a necessary element of the self-expression of redeemed man. Obviously, it is possible for man to pursue the conquest of the universe with complete disregard for the recovery of his relationship with God. But this may be less dangerous than for him to think that he can recover his authentic existence with God without ordering and perfecting that world which is part of his very being.

The specific witness which the Judaeo-Christian faith bears to this evolving world is the centrality of man in the process. Man must not be victimized by the scientific revolution; it must, on the contrary, serve to liberate him. And never may the dignity of the individual person be violated even for the sake of some great scientific conquest. No tyrant may build pyramids upon the corpses of human slaves.

III. This-Worldly Value of Eschatology

The danger of this happening, namely the inversion of cosmic values to the detriment of man, is all too real. It points up the importance — even from the point of view of human achievement — of the prophetic or eschatological witness of the Church. Granted that the other-worldly dimension of Christianity has been interpreted at times past as a call to retreat from the world, a complete swing to the other extreme is equally dangerous. Christianity is a healthy ferment in the world only when it keeps both seemingly contradictory poles — that of the marketplace and that of the desert, that of the Incarnation and that of the Parousia, the *here-and-now* and the *not-yet*.

Of the Church (and hence too of the world) the same principle holds as holds for the individual person. To love what I am *not-yet* is the only way to truly love what *I am*. For what *am* I but a *not-yet?* True, I have received much, I have acquired much, but my person, open as it must be to the infinite, is nothing more than a capacity to grow. The amazing thing about the growth of human personality is that when one's capacity is filled, it expands. I can love more, do more and receive more. In this world, all that *is* is also a *not-yet,* and any creature defies his own end the moment he forgets what he is not yet, to rest in what he is. It is true that I am good by what I am, but I am infinitely better by the not-yet latent in what I am. Because what I am is closer to me than my not-yet, the temptation is to love it more. But this is truly a temptation, for if I truly love what I am, I cannot be satisfied with what I am, for what I am is capable of growing (if I will let it), and one day I would like to say "I am" of what today I must say "I am not yet."

It hardly takes revelation to establish the truth that man's growth, his life, yes, his very existence, depends on his dynamic tension toward his "not yet." But it is something easily forgotten. Here the Church renders to the world the service of pointing beyond it. If this pointing beyond to the "not yet" seems at times inimical to the "now is," this is due to a misunderstanding, on the part of either the Church or the world, of the true meaning of Christian eschatology. Christian eschatology is not the eschatology of Leninism: the victory of the party at any price, even to the annihilation of human dignity. It is rather the proclamation of a goal that undergirds with transcendent force all that is human and cannot be achieved without the humanizing of man. What the Church proclaims to the world is that, like the individual personality, it cannot find itself unless it transcends itself.

Yet the Church is more than a mere static witness of eschatology to the world. She too, like the world, has her "now is" and her "not yet" in the very interior of her own being. And this leads her to a humble openness to the world. How can this be? The Church's longing for the Parousia is simply the not-yet dimension of her present being, which is also her being-in-the-world. She knows that the Parousia is not merely something to be awaited passively (or, biblically, in the attitude of sleep) but that it is also, in a very real sense, the fruit of her *immanent growth*. The realization that she is not yet there leads her to an openness to the world from which she may learn something of her Spouse who has left his traces there. In the voice of the world, its songs and its whimpers, she listens for the voice of the divine bridegroom who encounters her not merely from within her soul but also in the anonymous faces of mankind and speaks to her in the anonymous voices of the world. The Church thus strives not merely to serve the world and to give it a witness of transcendence, but also to listen to it. Her very ability and desire to listen is both the fruit and the sign of her eschatological longing, and in lending her ear to the world she by the very fact brings to the world a hope for its own renewal and life, a witness that there is a God who cares, because there is a God who listens.

The eschatological dimension of the Church does not deafen her ear to the voice of the world but makes it more sensitive. And this must also be true of the Church's great witness of celibacy. The celibate is a witness of eschatology to the Church, as the Church is a witness of eschatology to the world. But authentic celibacy is not a withering of this-worldly roots; it is not a plugging of this-worldly ears. Rather, assuming it is born of authentic love, celibacy screens out the foreground noises of its own personal this-worldly pursuits in order to listen to the agonizing cries of its brothers in the world, to be able to serve them more freely, to heal them and through this witness to remove the *if* in Paul's "If God be for us . . . " — or rather to show that the condition is not hypothetical but real. God is indeed for me, the world can say, because I have felt in the touch of a human hand the embrace of God.

IV. THE PROGRESSIVE NATURE OF REDEMPTIVE ACTION

Emerging out of all that has been said till now is the fact that the tension between the eschatological and the incarnational is really resolved in the comprehensive notion of an integral, "bodily" growth that is continual. Once it is seen that redemption involves the whole man, not just in the next world but already in this, then any action aimed at healing mankind and leading man to light and life — whether this be the physician's dedicated care or the diplomat's working for the international understanding, or the priest's absolution of the prodigal returning to the Father — all is part of an integral redemption. And when, furthermore, the redemption is conceived as a continually progressive thing, then the humblest physical restoration, because it is a humanizing and a personalizing act on the part of both minister and recipient is seen to be pregnant with the "greater yet" latent in this humble beginning — so that it can become, and indeed by its very nature is meant already to be — a sign and invitation (not to say a sacrament) of the encounter with the transcendent God and consummate fulfillment in him.

It may indeed not be seen that way from the recipient's side of the action — and it would be a mistake, through impatience on the part of the minister, to reveal prematurely the ultimate end to which the recipient's recovery (or new discovery) points. It would even tend to falsify the genuine value of the present degree of restoration to give the impression that the present renewal is *"only* a step" to a God not yet experienced. It may be a step, but it is not *only* a step. It is indeed real *life* that he has experienced, and until the patient himself feels, in the present acquisition, the thirst for the yet sweeter waters of life, it is best not to force them to his palate.

That is why, whatever the judgment the unbeliever makes of his motives, the Christian is really concerned, in fact anxiously concerned, with the immediate this-worldly value of his action and is truly disinterested in any further goal — if by this "interest" here is meant that the only reason the Christian gives a thirsty man a drink of water is in the hope that the man may ask for the last drops to be poured on his head in baptism. A "supernatural life" divorced from the natural bases would be no life at all.

On the other hand, to see man's fulfillment only in what "redemption" he has presently attained is to truncate and dehumanize him. For man's most fundamental and human factor is his openness to the ever-greater-yet, his openness to the infinite, an openness that is guaranteed only when it is thought of as terminating in nothing less than God. This at least is the Christian view. It would seem that here we have the real way out of the dilemma that dogs this whole question of the secular: if it is "supernatural" it is irrelevant; if it is "natural" then the universe and man himself is self-contained. But if we assume that in the concrete reality of things, all men have a transcendent destiny, then what is really crucial is their *openness* to grow, to achieve the "not yet" beckoning to them in their "is now." In other words, man's openness to the transcendent in and through each of his experiences is both the condition of his growth and the guarantor of relevance. Without such an openness to the transcendent, the very experience atrophies and frustrates. For in the heart of genuine existential encounter there must lie the realization that there is more here than I can now assimilate — there is mystery leading me on. Man must, like Moses looking from Nebo into the promised land, witness to more than he can grasp. Now the Christian view is that the thrust toward the infinite latent in every truly human desire, is really a thrust toward a Person, the infinite Person of God himself. The grandeur of the apostolate here on earth is that the divine Person who underlies every redeeming action is represented sacramentally, so to speak, by the visible human person in the human encounter.

But here a misconception must also be avoided. The Christian does not come to the world as someone outside it, to teach it something, to conquer it. The Christian becomes relevant to the world only when he first listens to it, and listens to it genuinely in order to learn. I think we would do well to explore the possibilities of a theology of the world as sacrament for the Christian. By this I mean that God and Christ can speak to us and shape us by speaking to us through the world — not only through nature but also through our fellowmen, whoever they may be. Is it not true that some of the greatest graces have come to us through some anonymous encounter in the world? If we are truly eager to hear his voice, we will be alert to hear it from any source. We will listen. And we will see Christ in the world. Not that we clothe the world with our image of Christ, superimposing it so to speak over all the filth — and loving the clothing without loving the person or the world we have clothed. This is a kind of religious narcissism that is indeed artificial and condescending. Rather, to love the world, to love men, is to respond truly to what they are and to what they can be. But we can never see what they truly are unless we believe there is something there to see, something we have not seen yet, something that we need for our own growth. In other words, we must not try to bring Christ to the world so much as to try to find him there. Or, better, we can bring Christ to the world only by finding him there.

Is this honestly possible? Is there a presence of God or Christ in the world of man to which we can genuinely respond? I think there is, and its scriptural basis is given in the Gospel of John. We are told in the prologue that the eternal Word enlightens *every man* (1:9). Now this could be taken proleptically of the illumination to be offered to the whole of mankind one day by the Incarnate Word. But the theology of the rest of the Gospel holds us to taking the expression seriously at face value. In 3:21, we read: "He who does the truth comes to the light, that his deeds may be manifest, for they have been performed in God."

Contrasted with those who refuse the light because their works are evil, those of whom John speaks here are certainly not yet Christians, for their "doing of the truth" precedes their coming to the light. Nevertheless prior to their even hearing about Christ, they are disposed toward him. Their works "have been performed in God," and therefore in grace. Illumined by the eternal Word in this anonymous divine encounter, they are disposed to accept the Incarnate Word if and when Providence arranges the encounter through the preaching of the Gospel, the example of Christian community, or whatever other channel. He to whom this happens will identify the good news of Christ as the fullness of the Light toward which he has been journeying. He will say: "This is what I've been looking for."

For John, the critical issue in man's salvation ("this is the judgment") is not, in the last analysis, being inside or outside the visible structure of the Church, but rather *what direction a man is going*. If he is moving toward the fullness of Light, even though because of historical accident he may still be outside it, he is already in John's terms "in God" or "of God" (3:21; 8:47) or "of the light" or "of the truth" (to Pilate, Jn 18:37). On the other hand, if he is moving away from it, no length of preaching, no method of persuasion will move him. For him the judgment has already taken place.

Now from this, two conclusions, it seems to me, follow inevitably. The first is that we should quit thinking of those in the Church and those outside it (or Church and World, if you wish) in static terms, as divided by the wall of Baptism — as if the whole story were told therewith. Much more meaningful and refreshing is it to think of belonging-to-the-Church in dynamic terms, in terms of the direction in which one is going. For, on the one hand, this approach heads off the self-righteous complacency which so easily infects those "who've made it" within the pale of visible salvation. And on the other hand, it opens up a real, unaffected solidarity with all those "on their way." We are joined in the kindly Light that is leading both of us on.

The second conclusion is simply an amplification of this latter point. If God is at work in the man "on the way," then it is quite possible that God has something to say to us *through him*. And thus we will have a real openness to listen and to learn from him. Better still, we will sense immediately that we are united in this Something that is "bigger than both of us," which is leading us on, and this realization makes possible the creation of real community between us. As Saint-Exupery once said of love, we will look not at each other, but we will look together in the same direction.

Obviously, the Church's approach to the world is a corporate work — diversified according to members. No one individual can exhaust all the possibilities of God's recreative action. Nor is it possible for the individual to work at all levels of redeeming activity at once. Some will manifest Christ's totally disinterested love to those who one knows already ahead of time will not requite in kind — the aged, the mentally retarded, the insane. Others will find in pagans or in those living a subhuman existence in our slums, the object of their loving solicitude and here too, they will be more interested in really loving them — and discovering how much of God is already in them! — than in "converting" them. Others will strive through education to lead men closer to the Light, conscious that even such a prosaic subject as mathematics can be an exercise of redemption if it leads to reverential openness and exigent fidelity to the truth. And so forth for every constructive human activity — and only constructive activity is human, just as only constructive activity is divine: "Love builds!"

V. THE SEMANTIC PROBLEM OF THE SCRIPTURES

We have said repeatedly that it is important for the Church to listen to the world. But what language is the world speaking today? Can we understand the language? And can we speak it in return?

Here we come to the most critical problem. The Church, having listened to the world, has something to say in return. But what does she have to say? And concerning the Scriptural message in particular (which is the aim of this study), how do we find out not merely what Scripture *meant* but also *what it means?*

If there is anything that emerged from our historical survey of the biblical theology of the secular, it was that at each stage of revelation we must distinguish between the cultural context of revelation and the formal thrust which it reveals within that context. Scripture itself is an evolving reality, and even the apostles "improved on," recast, adapted, added to and deleted from the words of Jesus as they encountered different milieux. Now did this process stop, as is often said, with the death of the last apostle? Rahner has shown how unconvincing it is to imagine that the constitution of revelation ceased mechanically at the very instant the last Apostle breathed his last. But even supposing a fluid date for the end of the apostolic age, there is something very inadequate about the image of the doors of heaven slamming shut, as if the "constitutive" period were now hermetically sealed off, only to be regarded as a revered relic by the outside world of continuing history. The facts of early Church history present quite a different picture. The canon was not settled until over 300 years after the writing of the Gospels. And even after that, up to the late Middle Ages, "Scripture" was understood to embrace not only the canon but the Fathers as well — in other words the living tradition which proclaimed the Word of God to each succeeding generation. Now this attitude reflects much more that of the apostles and of the sacred writers themselves in their handling of the traditional materials: not a slavery to the letter of a proposition but a concern that the relevant message of the Spirit reach the contemporary man in his specific situation.

Now if the Scriptures show that those who spoke authoritatively to the people of God at each stage of its development exercised a great freedom in reshaping and reinterpreting the earlier tradition to answer a new need or crisis — then what is to keep the Church today from doing the same? The "absolutist" will answer that revelation was *fixed* with the death of the last Apostle, and even though we admit a progress in revelation up to that point, not a jot or tittle may be changed since. But what if the essential lesson we find on every page of the Scriptures is that God at each age has something relevant to say — something that is often, because of cultural change, verbally different, if not even contradictory to an earlier statement in a different context? What if the lesson of Scripture is that God's heralds, including Jesus himself, latched on to whatever concepts were relevant to a given culture and used them to thrust man's thought *beyond* them to a new, more developed, more really divine insight — which is the *proper* or *formal* element in revelation? If this is true, what then *is* fidelity to the Scriptures if not to face our world without mental cobwebs — not with formulas mechanically repeated and only hopefully relevant — but with fresh and free formulations pouring forth from the boldness (*parrēsia*) which the Holy Spirit give the Church (Acts 4:13). It does not appear that we can be faithful to the very word of God we are trying to preserve unless we are willing to do so, even though this may mean speaking in terms different from those of the past and even at times from those of the Scriptures. This is not to negate the uniqueness of the witness of Scripture nor the once-for-all-ness either of the Christ-event or of the apostolic age. These were, in a sense, a summit which the Church ever strives to regain, a pristine experience which she ever tries to re-live. But re-*living* is not a traumatic withdrawal from the ongoing reality of the world in an endeavor to perpetuate a day gone forever — like the bride in Dickens' *Great Expectations* who shut herself up in the dining hall of the wedding banquet for which the groom never showed up, and lived to old maidenhood petrified in this world of fantasy. Re-living for the Church means discovering the thrust of the Spirit in each new age, and articulating it without slavery to the letter of the past.

This raises, of course, the critical question: "How far can you go in doing this?" How much of Scripture is perennial and how much is only cultural context? I assure you I'm not prepared to answer the question. Surely the Scripture scholars have a vital role in determining what Scripture *meant*. But the limits of saying what Scripture *means* are set not by the individual but by the Community to which and through which the Spirit speaks. This assumes a principle which is not subject to rational proof, namely that our contemporary *experience,* because of the abiding Spirit, is in basic *continuity,* if not identity, with that of the Apostolic Church. But our formulation of that experience need not, and often simply cannot be the same. In all of this the Church will, as she has always done, treasure the Scriptures and retain all of them. She will turn to them to find life, and she will insist that it is the message of *Scripture* she is proclaiming to the contemporary world. But the Church *hears* the Scriptures differently in each age; she finds a fresh meaning in them with the rise of each new generation. This is because each new generation *is* the Church of its age. The preaching of the Church is not some angelic voice *telling* an audience of mortals a message of God. Nor is it the continual replay of a record. Rather, it is the articulation of an experience which is indeed the experience of the paschal mystery but as it is experienced by contemporary man — for the Church lives, after all, only in the persons of contemporary men. Tradition, then, in its real sense is not a clinging to the formulas of the past, but a proclaiming of meaning in the present. Now while the role of the exegete and the historian is to fill in the picture so as to enable the Church to know *what it meant,* it is quite possible that for the unbelieving world and even for most Christians this is a process that is too time-consuming for them to pursue. They need to know the meaning of the message *now,* in language they can understand *now,* to resolve the problems they have *now.*

How can we who ponder the Scriptures more deeply translate them into relevance for others? The problem is significantly reduced if not solved, if they are meaningful to us first of all. But then the language of communication, we must never forget, is not merely one of words. It is also one of deeds. It is concrete action that the world understands best. Thus revelation through deeds continues

to be what it was in biblical times — the best way to con-
vince men of the reality of the living God. But the deeds
are not miraculous interventions of a *Deus ex machina;* rather
they are today the works of the Church, the living community
which continues the healing and reconciling and serving work
begun by the Servant of Yahweh and now inspired by the
risen Christ, the exalted Servant returned to the Father. The
works that are relevant and revelatory today will be those
that the world needs most — especially those of justice, peace,
and the unification of mankind, those, in short, spoken of
in the *Constitution on the Church in the Modern World.*

CONCLUSION

Such then are the thoughts I should like to offer *toward*
a biblical theology of the secular. The importance of "this
world" in the biblical message needs re-emphasis in our times.
However, a total identification of the people of God with
the world seems to be too simplistic a solution. It is not
sufficiently radical. The Church, while perpetually incarnating
herself in the world and in each new age, must remain a
creative agent even of worldliness. To do so, she needs to
witness to something *beyond* this world, to witness that we
have not here a lasting city. Our share in the city to come
depends indeed on how well we build this one. But we cannot build this one with freedom and genuine creative and
evolutionary thrust, unless we are possessed by the love that
builds without ceasing and without tiring, the love, in short,
whose other name is God.

Subject Index

Abraham, faith, 15
Alienation, fourfold, 19; healing of, 61, 72
Apocalyptic, 35 ff; imagery of, 51
Ascension, educative purpose, 47 f
Autonomy, from religion, 3

Battle Songs, 10 ff
Body, redemption and, 71 ff; redemption of, 60
Body of Christ, in Paul, 59 ff

Celibacy, eschatological witness, 28; expression of love, 66; and freedom, 57; and Holy War, 14; and involvement, 54 f, 75; and marriage, 56, 57; secular value of, 57; as witness, 55 ff
Christian life, incarnational and eschatological, 54 f
Church, diversification of works, 80; and meaning of Scripture, 83; and world, 79
Community, Christian, 48; and kingdom of God, 45; made by common ideal, 80
Covenant, and Holy War, 11; and king, 24; and kingdom of God, 24; and the secular, 7 ff
Creation, accounts of, 16 ff; in Babylonian mythology, 31; cosmic and historical, 34; and fall of Babylon, 32; new, to come, 34; and personalism, 33; return as new, 29 f; and salvation history, 33; speculation on, 30; theology of 2nd Isaiah, 30
Cross, in Paul's theology, 59
Cultural context, 49 f, 51 f, 53, 81 f

Day of the Lord, 37 f

Death, 20; covenant survives, 36
Death of Christ, and kingdom, 40
"Death of God," 1, 11 f
Desacralization, 9, 23, 69
Devil, exorcisms and kingdom, 42; see also Satan
Dualism, of Apocalyptic, 38

Elect, accept kingdom, 40
Eschatology, 27; and growth, 74; and marriage, 55; and present, 53; this-worldly value of, 73 f; witness to, 27
Eternal life, 38, 40, 49
Evolution, 69 f
Exile, 28 ff
Exodus, return as new, 28 f; and Yahweh's name, 5
Exorcism, sign of kingdom, 42

Fate, freedom from, 15
Freedom, 61; abuse of, 18; and celibacy, 57; from cosmic powers, 32; God's, 6; in involvement, 55, 65; in kerygma, 49; man's, 68 f; man's creative, 70
Future, functional, 41; and God, 68 ff; God and, 65; and Kingdom of God, 38, 40ff; and prophetism, 27; realization of present, 73; in revelation, 7; undetermined, 34
Fullness of Christ, 61 ff

God, alienation from, 20; "in a box," 36; "death of," 1; freedom of, 6, 7, 65 f, 68 f; functional, 37; and future, 68 ff; immanence, 7; independence of, 8, 15; involvement, 15; as judge, 39; and justice, 37; kingdom of, 9; love, 18; omnipotence, 37; personal, 14;

85

Biblical Index